THE FIELD GUIDE TO
YELLOWSTONE
AND
GRAND TETON
NATIONAL PARKS

KURT F. JOHNSON

FARCOUNTRY
PRESS

For my parents, who ignited the spark that
led to a life in wild places among wild things.

978-1-56037-555-5

© 2013 by Farcountry Press
Text and photography © 2013 by Kurt F. Johnson

Library of Congress Cataloging-in-Publication Data

Johnson, Kurt (Kurt F.)
   Field guide to Yellowstone and Grand Teton national parks / Kurt Johnson.
      pages cm
   Includes index.
   ISBN 978-1-56037-555-5 (softcover : alk. paper)
   1. Natural history--Yellowstone National Park. 2. Natural history--Wyoming-
-Grand Teton National Park. 3. Animals--Yellowstone National Park--Identifi-
cation.. 4. Animals--Wyoming--Grand Teton National Park--Identification.. 5.
Plants--Yellowstone National Park--Identification.. 6. Plants--Wyoming--Grand
Teton National Park--Identification.. I. Title.
   QH104.5.Y44J64 2013
   508.4787--dc23
                              2012046893

For more information about our books, write Farcountry Press, P.O. Box 5630,
Helena, MT 59604; call (800) 821-3874; or visit www.farcountrypress.com.

 Produced and printed in the United States of America.

25 24 23 22   6 7 8 9

Table of Contents

Introduction

The natural world is made up of so many different fascinating subjects that many of us find it difficult to pick one we would like to specialize in. This book was written by, and for, this sort of person: a naturalist. This term can apply to a professional career, but also refers to anyone who has a broad interest in the ecology around them, is a perpetual observer of the natural world, and who enjoys understanding not only the names of plants and animals, but how they connect to one another and to geological and ecological processes. I can't think of a better place to pay attention to these connections than the wilderness in and around Yellowstone and Grand Teton National Parks, which both offer a spectacular blend of dynamic geology, abundant wildlife, truly wild places, and contrasting seasons.

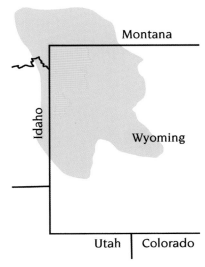

The Greater Yellowstone Ecosystem

The region covered in this book is commonly referred to as the Greater Yellowstone Ecosystem (GYE) and lies within the states of Wyoming, Montana, and Idaho (figure to left, outlined in green). There are many unique attributes to the GYE, but, ecologically, its most important characteristic is simply its large size. It is made up of approximately 18 million acres of mostly undeveloped public land. Yellowstone and Grand Teton National Parks lie within the heart of the GYE but represent only 14 percent of its total space. Most of the remaining land is managed by the USDA Forest Service, U.S. Fish and Wildlife Service, U.S. Bureau of Land Management, and state agencies. This abundance of undeveloped land allows predators such as grizzly bears, gray wolves, wolverines, and lynx to roam freely in this vast wilderness. The presence of these rare animals along with many other Rocky Mountain species has led to the GYE's oft-cited status as the only intact ecosystem in the contiguous United States. With the exception of the black-footed ferret, the GYE currently hosts the same spectrum of species that would have been found here before European settlement. Very few places in the world can make such a claim; human encroachment inevitably creates dramatic shifts in the natural world, often extirpating sensitive plants and animals.

Regularly, I have the very good fortune of seeing Yellowstone and Grand Teton National Parks through the eyes of first-time visitors. Every time I lead naturalist programs into these parks, I try to determine which aspects of the natural world will most interest each person. It is a safe bet that most people will be drawn to the "charismatic megafauna" such as bears, wolves, elk, and moose. But there are often more subtle interests as well, and I'm frequently surprised how many questions people have about things such as the grasses, insects, and reptiles found in this region.

The goal of this book is to provide identifications and descriptions for the most commonly encountered plants, animals, and geologic features of the GYE, including the more distinctive representatives. Due to the diversity of topics covered, this guide isn't comprehensive within any subject but aims to provide identifications and descriptions for species and features that are either most readily seen or are of particular interest. A fully comprehensive guide to this region would be enormous and include over 1,500 vascular plants, 10,000 species of insects, at least 318 species of birds, 10,000 geothermal features, and about 60 different mammals. If this guide does its job well, it will be an ideal companion in any backpack, canoe, or dashboard and will spark interest in the flora, fauna, and natural features of this amazing part of the world.

Land Overview within the Greater Yellowstone Ecosystem

Yellowstone National Park

Yellowstone has the unique status of being both a visually stunning national park to visit as well as a benchmark in the history of conservation. When Yellowstone was designated a national park in 1872 by President Ulysses S. Grant, the entire region was a vast and unsettled wilderness. The concept of a national park had never been fulfilled before, and considering that there was no shortage of open space at the time, this was a truly remarkable decision. Yellowstone served as the model for national parks throughout the United States, and for other countries as well. Today, there are an estimated 6,000 national parks around the world. Recent visitor surveys show that the primary reason for visiting Yellowstone is to view wildlife, but the original motivation for its creation was the unique concentration of geysers, hot springs, mudpots,

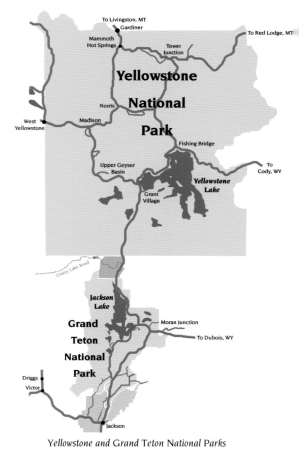

Yellowstone and Grand Teton National Parks

and waterfalls. Early explorers saw only a small percentage of the park's 10,000 geothermal features, but they recognized that this was a very unusual landscape. They also must have envisioned the potential for mismanagement without some form of protection. Today, Yellowstone spans 2.2 million acres in three states—Idaho, Montana, and Wyoming—with the vast majority of the park (about 96 percent) in Wyoming.

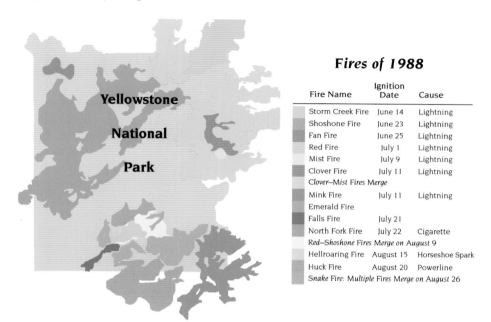

Fires of 1988

Fire Name	Ignition Date	Cause
Storm Creek Fire	June 14	Lightning
Shoshone Fire	June 23	Lightning
Fan Fire	June 25	Lightning
Red Fire	July 1	Lightning
Mist Fire	July 9	Lightning
Clover Fire	July 11	Lightning
Clover–Mist Fires Merge		
Mink Fire	July 11	Lightning
Emerald Fire		
Falls Fire	July 21	
North Fork Fire	July 22	Cigarette
Red–Shoshone Fires Merge on August 9		
Hellroaring Fire	August 15	Horseshoe Spark
Huck Fire	August 20	Powerline
Snake Fire: Multiple Fires Merge on August 26		

Often one of the first observations made by visitors to Yellowstone is the impact of wildfires on the park. Most of the visible burned areas are the result of an intense summer of fires that occurred in 1988 when over one third of the park burned to some degree. Evidence of these fires can be seen throughout the region. Despite the sense of disaster that such fires project, they offer interesting insight into the natural cycles of fires and forests. Wildfires occur every summer in and around Yellowstone and are an important force that clears debris, returns minerals to the soil, and benefits many plant and animal species. Most of the 1988 fires took place in lodgepole pine forests (by far the most common tree in the area), and almost all of the new growth within burned areas is also lodgepole pine. Read more about this tree's unique relationship with fire in the plant section of this book. Fire ecology may not be a primary reason for a visit to Yellowstone, but it is one of the more striking aspects of the park and certainly one of the most important.

Grand Teton National Park

The designation of the Teton Range and Jackson Hole as a national park is a bit more complicated than Yellowstone's story. Before becoming a national park, the mountains and forests of the Teton Range fell under the management of the USDA Forest Service, while most of the valley of Jackson Hole was privately owned. Plans for increased protection were offered as early as 1918, with proposals ranging from a southerly expansion of Yellowstone to allocating the valley of Jackson Hole as a national recreation area. These ideas were met with strong local opposition as concerns spread about grazing restrictions, the influx of tourists, and a loss of Western ambiance. The loudest voice in favor of national park designation was Horace Albright's, who became the first National Park Service superintendent of Yellowstone National Park in 1919. Despite his dedication to Yellowstone, Albright recognized the Tetons and Jackson Hole as equally worthy of preservation.

Initially, Albright's vision must have seemed unobtainable, but it moved closer to realization in 1926 when John D. Rockefeller Jr. visited Yellowstone and Jackson Hole. Albright personally guided Rockefeller throughout the valley with the hope of impressing the noted philanthropist. The gambit worked, and, with Albright's assistance, Rockefeller set out to purchase much of the private land of Jackson Hole with the intent of donating it to create a national park. This process also proved contentious, but Rockefeller was able to purchase a large portion of the valley and ultimately donated this land to the National Park Service. In 1943, President Franklin D. Roosevelt proclaimed Jackson Hole National Monument, absorbing Rockefeller's donated lands. The monument was then merged into Grand Teton National Park in 1950. This description oversimplifies what was a complicated and controversial process, but it demonstrates the strong emotions evoked by the landscapes of the GYE.

In its current size of almost 310,000 acres, Grand Teton National Park represents a small percentage of the GYE. Yet preservation of this distinct and dramatic landscape enables many present-day visitors to re-live Horace Albright's initial impression of this region by planning a visit based on Yellowstone's fame only to return home with equally memorable experiences from both national parks.

National Elk Refuge

The 24,700-acre National Elk Refuge is located in the southern portion of Jackson Hole. Managed by the U.S. Fish and Wildlife Service, this refuge was formally designated in 1912 with the primary purpose of providing winter range for elk and other mammals as well as habitat for breeding birds. A supplemental feeding program began a year earlier to prevent elk starvation and competition with domestic livestock, and continues today. Feeding wild elk has been a source of much debate with no easy answers. Continued feeding maintains a high population of elk but also concentrates the elk, which contributes to the spread of ungulate diseases such as brucellosis. Managers may consider future changes.

The National Elk Refuge is a wildlife mecca year-round but is especially interesting during winter when an average of 7,700 elk migrate onto the refuge for both natural forage and the supplemental feed. Most of the Jackson Hole bison herd also moves onto the refuge, as do predators and scavengers such as wolves, mountain lions, badgers, coyotes, golden eagles, and bald eagles.

National Forests

Yellowstone and Grand Teton National Parks may be the more celebrated lands within the GYE, but the vast majority of public land within the region is actually managed by the USDA Forest Service. Six national forests lie within this ecosystem and make up a total of over 14 million acres. These are the Bridger-Teton, Caribou-Targhee, Gallatin, Shoshone, Beaverhead, and Custer National Forests. Not all of this national forest land lies completely within the GYE, but it represents a significant portion of the area's wilderness and provides critical habitat for wildlife that roam large territories.

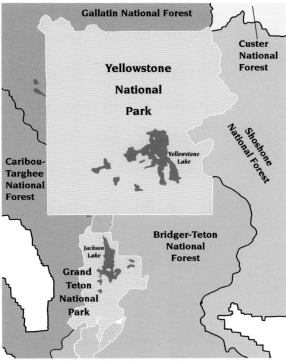

National Forests within the Greater Yellowstone Ecosystem (Beaverhead National Forest lies to the northwest of this map).

One Ecosystem, Many Mandates

The jurisdictional boundaries separating the various public lands are important to recognize because management policies and practices vary significantly among the different agencies. In general, national forests are managed as "multiple-use" lands: they support public recreation as well as industrial activities such as timber harvesting, mining, and grazing. A portion of each national forest in the GYE is formally designated as wilderness, off limits to most industrial uses; these are among the most pristine public lands in the world. Under the Organic Act of 1916, the National Park Service manages the parks "to conserve the scenery and the natural and historic objects and the wild life therein and to provide for the enjoyment of the same in such manner and by such means as will leave them unimpaired for the enjoyment of future generations." Commercial activities in the parks are limited to visitor and recreational services and sales. Finally, the mission of the U.S. Fish and Wildlife Service is "to conserve, protect, and enhance fish, wildlife, and plants and their habitats for the continuing benefit of the American people." Be aware of these sometimes overlapping, sometimes divergent management goals (and attendant regulations) as you travel around the GYE.

Climate

Weather in the GYE is notoriously unpredictable and sometimes extreme. It's important to be ready for any temperature and type of precipitation. The tables below show how weather varies considerably within the GYE, especially at different elevations. The difference in both temperature and precipitation between the bottom of a valley and a mountaintop can be surprising. For example, consider the average annual snow accumulation for the town of Jackson at 6,200 feet to the top of Jackson Hole Mountain Resort at over 10,000 feet. Even though these two locations are only ten miles apart, Jackson averages about 75 inches of snow per year, while the Mountain Resort receives an average of 475 inches.

Location	Avg. High Temp (F)				Avg. Low Temp (F)			
	Jan	Apr	Jul	Sep	Jan	Apr	Jul	Sep
Yellowstone (Overall)	28.6	49.4	79.6	67.8	9.6	26.0	46.7	37.0
Grand Teton (Overall)	25.7	49.0	80.0	68.9	1.2	22.1	41.2	32.2
Jackson, WY	27.5	52.5	81.9	71.1	5.4	24.7	40.6	31.5
West Yellowstone, MT	24.2	47.6	79.2	66.4	-0.2	19.7	35.3	29.4
Old Faithful	28.2	46.6	64.7	64.1	0.2	18.4	39.0	28.8
Cody, WY	35.9	56.8	84.9	72.2	12.8	31.4	54.7	43.4
Mammoth Hot Springs	29.2	49.5	79.9	67.5	10.3	26.2	46.9	37.5

Location	Avg. Precip. (Inches)					Avg. Snowfall (Inches)				
	Jan	Apr	Jul	Sep	Yr.	Jan	Apr	Jul	Sep	Yr.
Yellowstone (Overall)	1.1	1.2	1.5	1.3	15.4	14.5	5.9	0	0.5	72.1
Grand Teton (Overall)	2.6	1.5	1.2	1.4	21.3	44.4	9.3	0	0.5	177.0
Jackson, WY	1.5	1.1	1.1	1.3	15.9	20.2	3.9	0	0.1	74.7
West Yellowstone, MT	2.1	1.53	1.5	1.5	21.6	32.9	10.7	0	1.1	160.4
Old Faithful	2.3	2.1	1.7	1.5	24.4	38.6	20.2	0	1.7	212.4
Cody, WY	0.3	1.1	1.0	1.0	9.9	6.2	5.2	0	0.4	39.4
Mammoth Hot Springs	1.1	1.2	1.3	1.2	15.5	14.5	6.5	0	0.8	73.8

A Naturalist's Checklist

To fully experience the GYE's wildlife, plants, and other natural phenomena, you will find a few tools are a great complement to this field guide. The checklist below focuses on equipment related to the enjoyment of natural history. Remember to also bring bear spray, water, sunscreen, an insulating layer, and raingear.

- ☐ binoculars (8x45 is ideal for wildlife watching)
- ☐ small tape measure (for measuring tracks, etc.)
- ☐ hand magnifying lens (for seeing details in plants and insects)
- ☐ spotting scope (great for watching predators from long distances)
- ☐ camera (a perfect way to document an unknown plant or animal for later identification)*
- ☐ field notebook (great for documenting personal observations or for field sketches)
- ☐ headlamp with both white and red lenses (red light preserves night vision when looking at star charts)

* collecting plants, rocks, insects, or specimens of any kind is prohibited in national parks

Geology of the GYE

The geologic processes that formed today's landscape within the Greater Yellowstone Ecosystem (GYE) are some of the most dynamic and interesting on Earth. Visitors here see a land shaped by massive volcanic eruptions, mountain-building, seismic activity, and mountain-engulfing glaciers. Geologists continually discover new evidence to further illuminate the stories behind the natural features of the GYE. The primary purpose of this section is to provide identification guidance to the different types of rocks and minerals within the GYE, but we'll begin with a succinct description of some of the processes that have shaped this landscape.

The Yellowstone Supervolcano

As we watch Old Faithful erupt or go exploring the geyser basins within Yellowstone, one of the greatest, past and present, geologic forces of the area is quietly implied: an enormous heat source lies below us that drives these phenomena. Different theories have been proposed as to the origin of this heat source, but it is generally accepted that a volcanic hotspot of molten rock and magma lies below the surface of Yellowstone, originating more than 100 miles below and extending upward as close as 5 miles from the surface. This hotspot hasn't always been below Yellowstone. Evidence suggests that the hotspot originated in northern Nevada about 16 million years ago. As the North American plate moved to the southwest above the hotspot, a path of volcanic activity was left in its wake across southern Idaho. For the past 2 million years or so, Yellowstone has been

Huckleberry Ridge Caldera. 2.1 Million Years Ago
Henry's Fork Caldera. 1.3 Million Years Ago
Lava Creek Caldera. 640,000 Years Ago

Caldera-forming eruptions of Yellowstone.

home to volcanic activity ranging from relatively minor to catastrophic. Three major eruptions ejected massive amounts of ash and rock. The subsequent collapse of Earth's surface created enormous craters known as calderas. The first and largest of these eruptions occurred approximately 2.1 million years ago and formed the Huckleberry Ridge Caldera. This caldera's rim has mostly eroded over time so its boundaries are

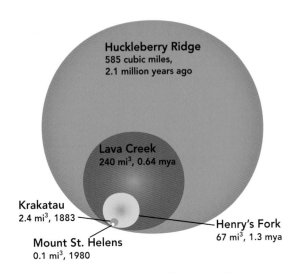

Huckleberry Ridge
585 cubic miles,
2.1 million years ago

Lava Creek
240 mi³, 0.64 mya

Krakatau
2.4 mi³, 1883

Mount St. Helens
0.1 mi³, 1980

Henry's Fork
67 mi³, 1.3 mya

Comparison of past volumes of volcanic eruptions.

less defined, but the eruption itself is considered to be one of the Earth's largest in the past few million years. The ash from this single eruption probably darkened the skies around the world and lowered global temperatures by several degrees.

After a period of relative dormancy, a smaller eruption to the west of Yellowstone 1.3 million years ago created the Henry's Fork Caldera. This was followed by an eruption 640,000 years ago that was between the first two in size, creating the Lava Creek Caldera. Being the most recent of the three major eruptions, this caldera's rim has eroded the least and measures roughly 45 miles wide and 30 miles long. The extent of this caldera is clearly depicted on the Yellowstone visitor map that rangers hand out at park entrances and visitor centers.

Due to the enormous volcanic potential that lies beneath Yellowstone, geologists pay careful attention to this region. One of the unusual characteristics that can be measured is the amount of "caldera breathing," or the constant swelling and collapsing of the caldera floor. This movement is very atypical for the Earth's surface; it uplifted the caldera as much as three feet between the 1920s and 1980s. The volcanic activity beneath Yellowstone generates almost daily seismic activity, most of which is small and detectable only by precise instruments. Big seismic events are still possible. In August 1959, a 6.3-magnitude earthquake followed immediately by a 7.5 earthquake rattled the mountains just west of Yellowstone. The shaking was felt throughout the region and caused many of Yellowstone's geothermal features to behave abnormally. The quake also generated a landslide that killed 28 people outside the park and blocked the Madison River, creating Quake Lake. Damage was widespread and totaled millions of dollars. Such dynamic geologic forces also spawn episodes of sensational media attention because geologists generally believe that Yellowstone will someday erupt violently once again. Fortunately, experts also believe this is unlikely to occur any time soon.

The Tetons and Jackson Hole

It is certain that anyone who gazes upon the Teton Range will be inspired in some way. These mountains stir us to climb them, photograph them, enjoy the creatures found within their shadows, and to simply slow down and appreciate the dramatic wildness they represent. At even the briefest glance, the Tetons demonstrate that tremendous geologic processes are at work. As with so much of the natural world, when we look closer the story becomes even more impressive.

In contrast to Yellowstone's volcanic history, the Tetons were shaped largely by millions of years of seismic activity occurring along a fault between the mountains' base and the valley floor. The elevational difference between Jackson Hole's valley floor and the Tetons' highest peak, the Grand Teton, is about 7,000 feet. But at 13,770 feet, the "Grand" isn't an especially tall mountain by Rocky Mountain standards; it isn't even the tallest peak in Wyoming (this superlative is held by 13,804-foot Gannett Peak in the Wind River Range). The primary characteristic that makes the Grand Teton and its surrounding peaks so incredibly dramatic is the fact that, unlike most mountain ranges, it lacks gradual foothills on its eastern front and instead rises abruptly thousands of feet into the sky. Considering that the Tetons didn't begin their growth until 13 to 10 million years ago, they simply haven't had much time, on a geologic scale, to erode.

The fault mentioned above is referred to as a "normal" fault, which means that two large blocks of earth are pulling apart. One block (the valley) slips downward, while the other (the Tetons) rises. Tension builds along the fault line and is periodically released through earthquakes. The potential for earthquakes is still a serious concern to this portion of the GYE; the fault could produce up to a 7.5-magnitude quake. This is why Teton County, which includes the city of Jackson, has rigid codes for new construction and why $82 million was spent to reinforce Jackson Lake Dam in the 1980s.

The diagram below depicts the fault blocks pulling away from one another in purple. But one of the most interesting aspects of this mountain-building process is revealed by studying the thick layer of sediments that have filled the valley as a result of glaciation, deposition from the Snake River, past volcanism, and erosion of the surrounding landscape. Taking these sediments into account shows that an initial—and logical—deduction that the fault displaced these blocks 7,000 feet is incorrect because as much as 16,000 of feet of sediment has filled the valley floor over time! This means that the real distance achieved as the valley side of the fault dropped and the mountain side of the fault rose is closer to a difference of 23,000 feet.

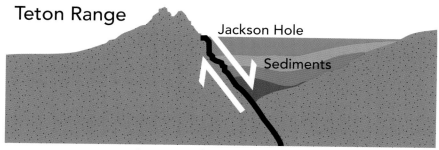

Cross section of the Teton fault and valley fill.

Glaciation within the Greater Yellowstone Ecosystem

Map of the Bull Lake Glaciation (lighter blue), which peaked about 140,000 years ago, and the Pinedale Glaciation (darker blue), which peaked about 19,000 to 15,000 years ago.

Past glaciations can be thought of as the most recent ingredient added to the recipe that created the current landscape of the region. Enormous glaciers originating in the high plateau of Yellowstone covered the area with thousands of feet of ice and stretched well beyond both parks' current boundaries. There were many periods of advancing and retreating ice, but two of these, the Bull Lake and Pinedale Glaciations, occurred relatively recently within the GYE and consequently left more obvious evidence of their presence. The Bull Lake Glaciation may have begun as much as 150,000 years ago and continued until about 40,000 years ago. This was an extended period of cold temperatures during which falling snow accumulated year-round at high elevations, forming a thick glacial ice cap over Yellowstone. Extensive glaciers also formed in the Teton, Gros Ventre, and Absaroka Ranges. Jackson Hole would have experienced an influx of glaciers from the north, east, and west, filling the entire valley with 2,000 to 3,000 feet of ice.

After an interglacial period of warming, temperatures cooled again allowing the Pinedale Glaciation to dominate the region. The quantity and extent of glacial ice associated with this period was almost as substantial as the Bull Lake period, but didn't extend as far south or west. Advances of these glaciers created several notable features of today's landscape: Jackson Lake, the extensive terminal moraine (large pile of debris deposited at the furthest extent of a glacier) just north of the Snake River Overlook known as Burned Ridge, and much of the overall topography of Jackson Hole. Toward the end of the Pinedale Glaciation, each canyon within the Teton Range would have filled with ice continually creeping downhill toward the

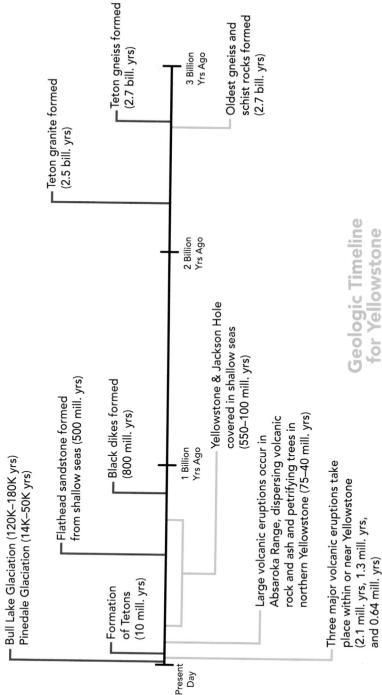

Geologic Timeline for Tetons and Jackson Hole

Bull Lake Glaciation (120K–180K yrs)
Pinedale Glaciation (14K–50K yrs)

Flathead sandstone formed from shallow seas (500 mill. yrs)

Black dikes formed (800 mill. yrs)

Teton granite formed (2.5 bill. yrs)

Teton gneiss formed (2.7 bill. yrs)

Oldest gneiss and schist rocks formed (2.7 bill. yrs)

Present Day

1 Billion Yrs Ago

2 Billion Yrs Ago

3 Billion Yrs Ago

Formation of Tetons (10 mill. yrs)

Geologic Timeline for Yellowstone

Yellowstone & Jackson Hole covered in shallow seas (550–100 mill. yrs)

Large volcanic eruptions occur in Absaroka Range, dispersing volcanic rock and ash and petrifying trees in northern Yellowstone (75–40 mill. yrs)

Three major volcanic eruptions take place within or near Yellowstone (2.1 mill. yrs, 1.3 mill. yrs, and 0.64 mill. yrs)

The Teton Glacier as seen to the right and below the Tetons' highest peak, the Grand Teton.

valley floor where it then spread out laterally. The force behind each of these valley glaciers was enough to scour out large depressions and leave moraines at the terminal and lateral edges. When standing along the east shore of Jenny Lake, a terminal moraine is beneath your feet as you look across at the previously glacier-filled Cascade Canyon and the depression at its base which is Jenny Lake itself.

Glaciation is primarily studied by the evidence left behind from thousands of years ago. In the Tetons, however, a handful of glaciers remain today and can be seen on a clear day. In the northern section of the Tetons, Skillet and Falling Ice Glaciers can be seen on Mount Moran, while Teton Glacier is the easiest to see among the highest peaks. Like most glaciers around the world, Teton Glacier is receding. Its total length as of 2009 was estimated to be about 1,500 feet and it is receding an average of 30 feet per year.

The diagram on the next page shows how, in active glaciers such as those in the Tetons, there is a zone of accumulation (gain of ice) and a zone of ablation (loss of ice). The relationship between these two zones determines whether a glacier is advancing or retreating.

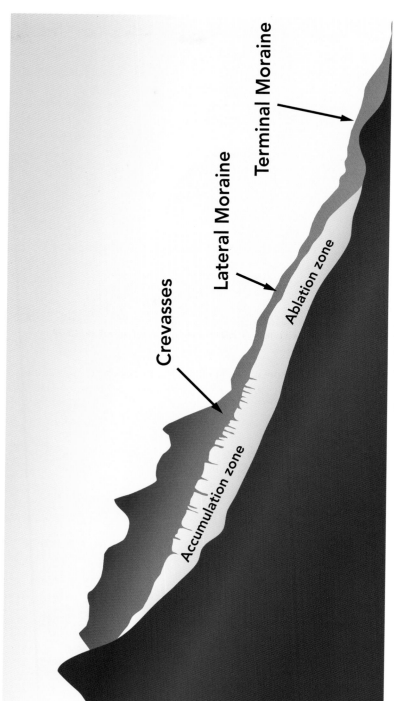

Cross section of a glacier.

Minerals

Minerals are the basic materials that make up different rock types. There are over 4,000 different types of minerals on Earth, but the varieties described on this page comprise the vast majority found in the field. Quartz and feldspar alone make up about 90 percent of all minerals. The hardness is based on a scale of 1 to 10 with 1 being relatively soft and 10 being as hard as a diamond.

Quartz
Hardness: 7

Orthoclase Feldspar
Hardness: 6

Plagioclase Feldspar
Hardness: 6

Biotite Mica
Hardness: 2.5

Calcite
Hardness: 3

Hornblende
Hardness: 5

Olivine
Hardness: 6.5 to 7

Dolomite
Hardness: 3 to 4

Serpentine
Hardness: 3 to 5

Chlorite
Hardness: 2.5

Igneous Rocks

Igneous rocks have been solidified from molten magma. Some magma cools underground, forming rocks such as granite, and other magma erupts to the Earth's surface, forming rocks such as basalt. The mineral grains within this rock type range from microscopic to inches in length. Igneous rocks are found in many areas throughout the GYE, but sites closest to Yellowstone's past volcanic eruptions are the best locations to see some of these rocks.

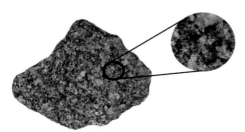

Granite
Consists primarily of quartz and feldspar with flecks of other dark minerals, especially biotite.

Obsidian
Dark, glassy rock that cooled instantly as it erupted.

Layers of columnar basalt near Tower Falls, Yellowstone.

Basalt
Dark, solidified lava flows.

Gabbro
Same minerals as basalt, but with coarser grains due to slower cooling underground.

Grand Canyon of the Yellowstone River with surrounding rhyolite rock.

Pumice
Lightweight and porous.
Formed from quickly cooling
gaseous magma.

Rhyolite
Gray to pink.
Common in Yellowstone.

Andesite
Lighter-colored
volcanic rock.

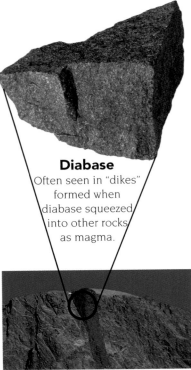

Diabase
Often seen in "dikes"
formed when
diabase squeezed
into other rocks
as magma.

Scoria
Basalt made porous due
to release of gas
while cooling.

*Mount Moran in the northern Teton Range
has a distinct diabase dike running
vertically through the peak.*

Metamorphic Rocks

Metamorphic rocks have been subjected to pressure and heat deep underground. These forces have changed them from their "parent rock" into their current state. Any rock may eventually become a metamorphic rock under the right conditions, altering the structure without melting the rock.

Slate
Foliated (aligned in parallel planes); may split into layers.

Marble
Usually non-foliated rock formed from limestone or dolostone. Not very common in GYE.

Quartzite
Formed from sandstone. These very hard rocks are rounded by tumbling in rivers and glaciers. Quartzite cobble covers the valley floor of Jackson Hole.

Gneiss
Formed from many different rock types. Foliated with alternating dark and light bands of minerals. May look similar to granite but has layers.

Schist
Formed from shale. Foliated and shiny due to high concentrations of mica.

Along with granite, schist and gneiss
compose the core of the Teton Range.

Sedimentary Rocks

Sedimentary rocks are deposited as layers of rock grains formed by erosion or as deposits precipitated from water. These processes take place on the Earth's surface, and sedimentary deposits account for about 75 percent of rocks found on our planet's surface. Sedimentary layers are also important sources of oil and coal.

Sandstone
A common rock formed of layers of sand deposited by water or wind. Grains are visible to the naked eye. Example on left has reddish color from iron-coated sand grains.

Travertine
Carbonate deposits resulting from hot springs.

Travertine terraces at Mammoth Hot Springs.

Limestone
Calcium carbonate formed by the deposition of marine organisms or precipitated from water.

Chert
Very small crystals and high concentrations of silica.

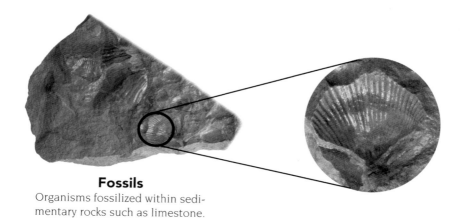

Fossils
Organisms fossilized within sedimentary rocks such as limestone.

Petrified Wood
Forests in northern Yellowstone were petrified when silica-rich volcanic mudflows encased the trees and minerals replaced the trees' organic tissue.

Conglomerate
Coarse rocks with rounded pebbles cemented together by fine grains.

Coal
Organic carbon from buried plants. Usually black and shiny.

Shale
Soft, fine-grained rock made of clay and mud.

Geothermal Features of the GYE

Yellowstone National Park is home to the greatest concentration of geothermal features in the world. The presence of these phenomena so impressed the region's first visitors they sparked the efforts that eventually led to its designation as the world's first national park in 1872. About 10,000 geothermal features are found within Yellowstone and each one falls within one of four categories: geysers, mudpots, fumaroles (steam vents), and hot springs. Geothermal features such as these require sufficient water, a significant heat source, and the right kind of "plumbing" within the rock below. The water source is Yellowstone's average of 15 inches of precipitation per year. Much of that rain and snowmelt eventually drains underground and is superheated (reaching temperatures up to 400°F) by the magma chamber beneath the region. The hot water and steam make their way upward, passing through beds of rhyolite, the dominant rock type beneath geyser basins. This igneous rock is porous and high in silica content. Some of this silica dissolves in the hot water and coats the cracks and fissures within the rhyolite, creating a high-pressure plumbing system that funnels the water toward the surface.

The illustration below shows the different ways that this hot water can manifest itself on the surface. If it meets a constriction before reaching the surface, pressure builds up and the water periodically releases in the form of a geyser. A cone geyser has a deposit of silica around its opening (called geyserite), while a fountain geyser typically erupts (serious geyser-gazers would say "plays") from a pool. In the absence of a constriction, the water may surface directly as a hot spring (the most common thermal feature in the park), as a fumarole that lacks sufficient water to pool, or as a mudpot, which contains acidic water and consequently breaks down the surrounding rock and forms bubbling pools of viscous mud.

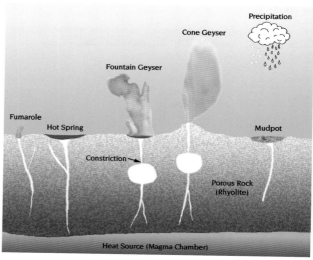

The geothermal features within this region possess their own unique beauty, but it is critical to understand that most of them can also be deadly. While exploring Yellowstone and its many geothermal areas, stay on designated boardwalks and trails. Hot springs have claimed too many lives and caused too many injuries throughout Yellowstone's past. Please respect all warnings, and know that unsigned areas may also be lethal.

Upper Geyser Basin

The Upper Geyser Basin is home to the world's most famous geyser, Old Faithful, and more than 200 others, about one fifth of all geysers in the world. Updated eruption predictions for several geysers are posted in the Old Faithful Visitor Center, where you can also obtain a free handout called "Current Geysers." This is a helpful guide as geyser characteristics change over time.

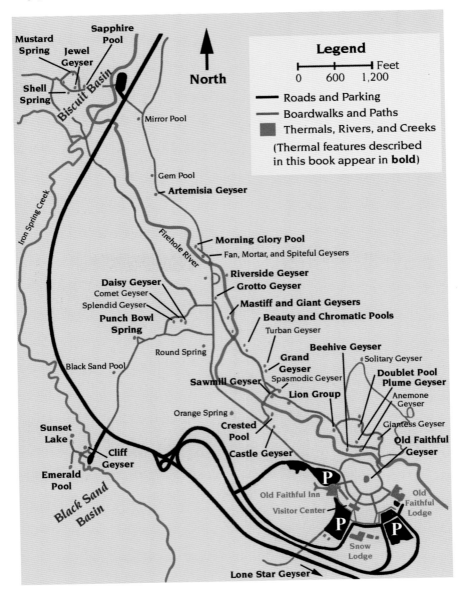

Lone Star Geyser

- interval: 3 hours
- duration: 30 minutes
- height: 30 to 45 feet
- extremely large cone (over 9 feet tall), loud and powerful eruption is well worth the 2.5-mile hike along upper Firehole River
- trailhead is just south of Kepler Cascades, south of the Old Faithful area. Easy trail follows old roadbed; bicycles allowed

Old Faithful Geyser

- interval: 50 to 127 minutes (93 minutes on average)
- duration: 1.5 to 5 minutes
- height: 106 to 184 feet
- discharge: 3,700 to 8,400 gallons
- 72 feet below surface, water is super-heated to 244°F. The vent opening at the surface is 1.5x3 feet, but 22 feet down, the "plumbing" narrows to only 4 inches

Beehive Geyser

- interval: hours to days (usually over 20 hours)
- duration: 4 to 5 minutes
- height: 150 to 200 feet
- unpredictable but has an "indicator" spout to the south, which almost always predicts a Beehive eruption within 10 minutes

Plume Geyser

- interval: 25 to 45 minutes
- duration: 1 to 2 minutes
- height: 10 to 30 feet
- characteristics change frequently; experiences periods of dormancy

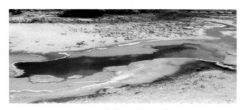

Doublet Pool

- temperature: 194°F
- depth: 8 feet
- this spring is actually two connected pools surrounded by a fragile ledge

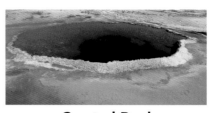

Crested Pool

- temperature: 199°F
- depth: 42 feet
- experiences occasional surges of bubbles

Lion Geyser Group

- interval: 2 to 5 hours
- duration: 2 to 6 minutes
- height: 30 to 60 feet
- this complex of four geysers consists of Little Cub, Big Cub, Lioness, and (the most distinct) Lion Geyser

Sawmill Geyser

- interval: 1 to 3 hours
- duration: 15 to 90 minutes
- height: 5 to 40 feet

Castle Geyser

- interval: about 13 hours
- duration: 15 to 20 minutes
- height: 30 to 100 feet
- large cone (over 12 feet tall) suggests that Castle has been erupting for thousands of years

Grand Geyser

- interval: 8 hours
- duration: 8 to 12 minutes
- height: 160 to 200 feet
- tallest predictable geyser in the world
- strongly associated with nearby Vent and Turban Geysers

Beauty & Chromatic Pools

- temperature: 168°F
- depth: 25 feet
- Beauty (top) and Chromatic (bottom) are connected and control one another's depths

Mastiff Geyser

- interval: variable
- duration: variable
- height: 1 to 30 feet

Giant Geyser

- duration: up to an hour
- height: 150 to 250 feet (second only to Steamboat Geyser)
- relatively inactive since the 1950s with only periodic and unpredictable eruptions
- eruptions often associated with Mastiff Geyser

Grotto Geyser

- interval: variable
- duration: 3 to 13 hours
- height: 3 to 30 feet
- the geyserite rock surrounding this geyser probably originated from petrifying tree stumps

Riverside Geyser

- interval: 5 to 8 hours
- duration: 20 minutes
- height: 75 feet
- usually erupts 20 minutes before or 25 minutes after the predicted time
- one of the most beautiful geysers (often accompanied by a rainbow)

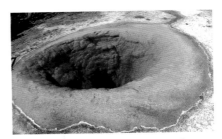

Morning Glory Pool

- temperature: 171°F
- depth: 23 feet
- a colorful and iconic Yellowstone feature
- its popularity led to many coin donations, which altered its coloration; 8,627 pennies and other debris were recovered from its depths in 1950

Artemisia Geyser

- interval: 6 to 16 hours
- duration: 10 to 30 minutes
- height: 10 to 25 feet
- this is a very large geyser crater with deep blue water
- the infrequent eruptions are impressive and long-lasting

Daisy Geyser

- interval: 1.5 to 2 hours
- duration: 3 to 4 minutes
- height: 75 feet
- one of the most predictable geysers and closely associated with Splendid Geyser

Punch Bowl Spring

- temperature: 199°F
- depth: 30 feet
- probably was a geyser in the past; now a hot spring with distinct ridges

Living Color

The vibrant colors in Yellowstone's hot springs come from *thermophiles*—bacteria and other microbes that thrive in hot water. Gradations of colors denote different types of thermophiles, each with their own preferred temperature range. Vivid blues are the exception. When sunlight hits deep, clear water, the blue light waves scatter more than other colors, bouncing the blue back to our eyes.

Thermophiles are also sensitive to a spring's acidity and chemical make-up. Some species live only in acidic water, some only in alkaline water, and others require sulphur or calcium carbonate. Colonies of billions of microbes may form a thin coating (called a sinter) or thicker mats on the water's surface, while other species cluster in string-like "streamers" and vertical columns or pedestals. Scientists have found that some microbes even migrate within their colonies in response to changing temperatures and other conditions.

Black Sand Basin

Emerald Pool
* temperature: 155°F
* depth: 25 feet
* the beauty of this pool is due to its dark green waters surrounded by bright orange bacterial mats

Sunset Lake
* temperature: 180°F
* depth: 24 feet
* this huge pool is mostly dormant but occasionally erupts up to 30 feet high

Cliff Geyser
* interval: variable but frequent
* duration: variable
* height: 10 to 20 feet

Biscuit Basin

Jewel Geyser

- interval: 5 to 15 minutes
- duration: 1 to 2 minutes
- height: 10 to 30 feet
- erupts regularly but affected by seismic activity

Mustard Spring

- relatively dormant as a geyser, but periodically erupts up to 10 feet for a few minutes

Sapphire Pool

- temperature: 200°F
- mostly dormant, but shortly after the 1959 earthquake, erupted up to 125 feet

Shell Spring

- erupts infrequently up to 6 feet high and lasts up to an hour

Gibbon (Artist Paint Pot) Geyser Basin

Artist Paint Pots

- located south of Norris Junction
- 0.5 mile from the trail-head, this feature is well worth the short hike
- texture and consistency resemble a painter's palette
- constantly bubbling and shooting mud several feet up into the air

Midway Geyser Basin

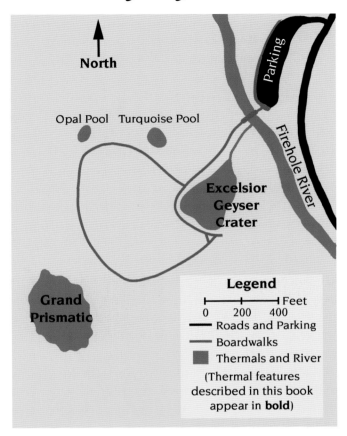

North

Opal Pool   Turquoise Pool

Parking

Firehole River

Excelsior Geyser Crater

Grand Prismatic

Legend

├──────┼──────┤ Feet
0   200   400

── Roads and Parking

── Boardwalks

■ Thermals and River

(Thermal features described in this book appear in **bold**)

Grand Prismatic

- temperature: 147° to 188°F
- discharge: 560 gallons per minute
- this is Yellowstone's largest, and to many, its most beautiful hot spring
- considered to be the third-largest hot spring in the world

Excelsior Geyser Crater

- temperature: 199°F
- discharge: over 4,000 gallons per minute
- in its prime, this may have been Yellowstone's largest geyser
- in the late 1800s, a hydrothermal explosion created the large (and mostly dormant) geyser crater we see today

Lower Geyser Basin

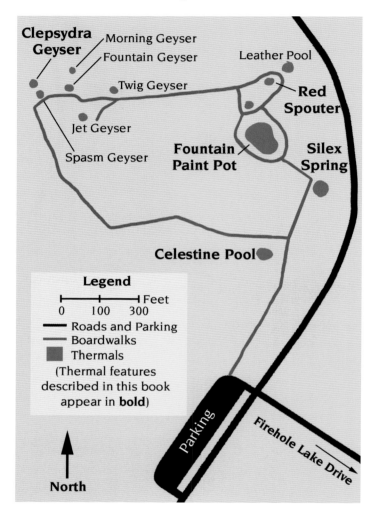

Clepsydra Geyser

Morning Geyser

Fountain Geyser

Leather Pool

Twig Geyser

Red Spouter

Jet Geyser

Spasm Geyser

Fountain Paint Pot

Silex Spring

Celestine Pool

Legend

			Feet
0	100	300	

— Roads and Parking
— Boardwalks
■ Thermals
(Thermal features described in this book appear in **bold**)

↑ North

Parking

Firehole Lake Drive

Celestine Pool

- typically dormant but can erupt up to a few feet
- this 200°F pool was the site of a horrible incident in 1981 when a dog jumped in and its owner jumped in after it, killing both

Silex Spring

- temperature: 193°F
- depth: 27 feet
- deep blue centrally with radiating orange and yellow thermophiles (heat-loving microbes)

Fountain Paint Pot

- temperature: 203°F
- this colorful mudpot is acidic, which breaks down the surrounding silica-rich soil

Spring

Red Spouter

- unique feature that transforms from a muddy hot spring to a mudpot and then to a steam vent as summer progresses

Fall

Clepsydra Geyser

- duration: continuous
- height: 10 to 45 feet
- experiences periods of inactivity but generally erupts non-stop

Firehole Lake Drive

White Dome Geyser
- interval: 12 to 24 minutes but variable
- duration: 2 to 3 minutes
- height: 10 to 30 feet
- this is one of the largest geyser cones in Yellowstone (about 12 feet high)

Firehole Lake & Hot Lake
- these two large thermal pools are located adjacent to one another on the far east side of Firehole Lake Drive

Great Fountain Geyser
- interval: 12 hours
- duration: 45 to 60 minutes
- height: 75 to 200 feet
- once overflow from the vent is seen, an eruption typically occurs within 1 to 2 hours

Pink Cone Geyser
- interval: 6 to 16 hours
- duration: 2 to 3 minutes
- height: 20 to 35 feet
- activity increased following the region's 1959 earthquake

Norris Geyser Basin

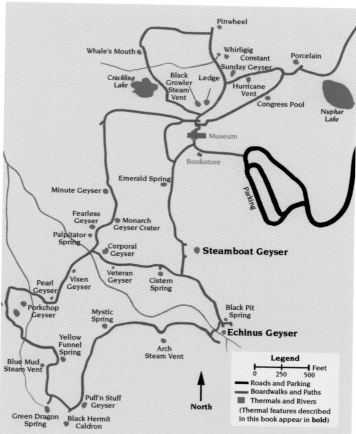

Pinwheel

Whale's Mouth

Whirligig
Constant
Sunday Geyser

Porcelain

Crackling
Lake

Black
Growler
Steam
Vent

Ledge

Hurricane
Vent

Congress Pool

Nuphar
Lake

Museum

Bookstore

parking

Emerald Spring

Minute Geyser

Fearless
Geyser

Monarch
Geyser Crater

Palpitator
Spring

Corporal
Geyser

Steamboat Geyser

Veteran
Geyser

Cistern
Spring

Pearl
Geyser

Vixen
Geyser

Porkchop
Geyser

Mystic
Spring

Black Pit
Spring

Echinus Geyser

Yellow
Funnel
Spring

Arch
Steam Vent

Blue Mud
Steam Vent

Legend

| 0 | 250 | 500 | Feet |

━━ Roads and Parking
━━ Boardwalks and Paths
■ Thermals and Rivers
(Thermal features described
in this book appear in **bold**)

Puff'n Stuff
Geyser

North

Green Dragon
Spring

Black Hermit
Caldron

Steamboat Geyser

- interval: months to years, much more frequent as of 2018
- height: 10 to 350 feet
- not predictable but considered to be the tallest geyser in the world

Echinus Geyser

- interval: variable
- height: 50 to 100 feet
- very active up until 2001; now more dormant and unpredictable

West Thumb Geyser Basin

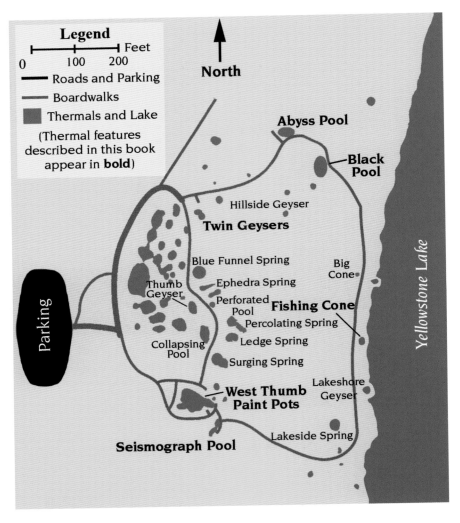

Legend

Feet

0   100   200

— Roads and Parking

— Boardwalks

▓ Thermals and Lake

(Thermal features described in this book appear in **bold**)

↑ **North**

Abyss Pool

Black Pool

Hillside Geyser

Twin Geysers

Blue Funnel Spring

Big Cone

Thumb Geyser

Ephedra Spring

Perforated Pool

Fishing Cone

Percolating Spring

Collapsing Pool

Ledge Spring

Surging Spring

Lakeshore Geyser

West Thumb Paint Pots

Seismograph Pool

Lakeside Spring

Parking

Yellowstone Lake

Seismograph Pool

- a relatively cool thermal pool. Once known as Blue Pools, the name was changed after the 1959 earthquake

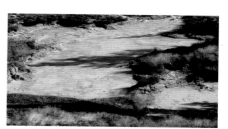

West Thumb Paint Pots

- temperature: 190 to 199°F
- this wide mudpot (about 30 feet in diameter) is constantly bubbling and one of the more dynamic sights in this basin

Fishing Cone

- temperature: 170°F
- this unique feature gained notoriety for its location on the shores of Yellowstone Lake where (according to some) fish could be caught and immediately cooked in its near-boiling waters

Black Pool

- temperature: 170°F
- depth: 30 feet
- the lower temperature of this pool allows for darker cyanobacteria to thrive, giving it a murky yet beautiful coloration

Abyss Pool

- temperature: 172°F
- depth: 53 feet
- one of the larger and deeper pools in Yellowstone that has erupted as a geyser in the past; generally dormant in recent years

Twin Geysers

- interval: variable
- height: up to 120 feet
- historically this is the largest geyser at West Thumb; mostly dormant since the 1970s

Mammoth Hot Springs

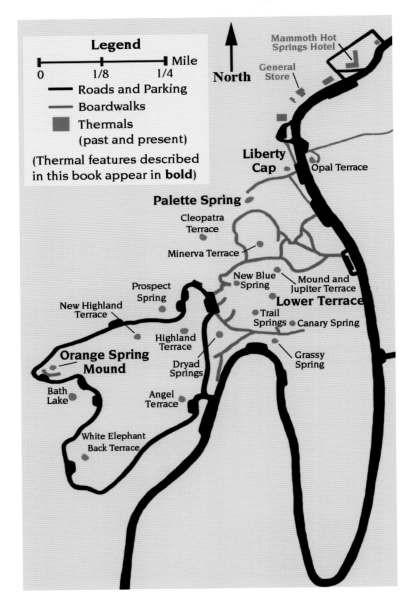

Legend

Mile
0   1/8   1/4

North

Roads and Parking
Boardwalks
Thermals
(past and present)

(Thermal features described
in this book appear in **bold**)

Mammoth Hot
Springs Hotel

General
Store

**Liberty
Cap**

Opal Terrace

Palette Spring

Cleopatra
Terrace

Minerva Terrace

New Blue
Spring

Mound and
Jupiter Terrace

Prospect
Spring

Lower Terrace

New Highland
Terrace

Trail
Springs

Canary Spring

Highland
Terrace

**Orange Spring
Mound**

Dryad
Springs

Grassy
Spring

Bath
Lake

Angel
Terrace

White Elephant
Back Terrace

Palette Spring

- a steep terrace with wonderful colors due to thermophilic activity
- named for the variety of hues reminiscent of an artist's palette
- this terrace has exhibited various levels of color and thermal activity and was dry for much of the early 1900s

Lower Terrace

- the many terraces within the Mammoth area; made of enormous travertine (calcium carbonate) steps, are some of Yellowstone's most iconic features
- Mammoth's terraces change frequently; collectively, geothermal activity deposits two tons of minerals each day

Orange Spring Mound

- temperature: 157°F
- gray travertine beautifully streaked with orange-colored thermophile bacteria
- an 1880s photograph shows this terrace was then about two thirds of its current height

Liberty Cap

- height: 37 feet
- now inactive but historically had a source of mineral-rich water that left extensive travertine deposits over time
- named for its resemblance to caps worn in the French Revolution, this distinct cone is estimated to be more than 2,000 years old

The Mud Volcano Area

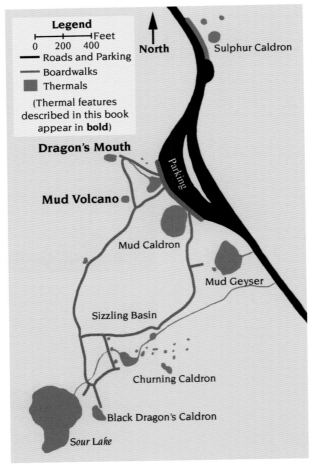

Legend

|———|———|Feet
0   200   400
—— Roads and Parking
—— Boardwalks
■ Thermals

(Thermal features described in this book appear in **bold**)

North

Sulphur Caldron

Dragon's Mouth

Parking

Mud Volcano

Mud Caldron

Mud Geyser

Sizzling Basin

Churning Caldron

Black Dragon's Caldron

Sour Lake

Dragon's Mouth

- temperature: 170°F
- this murky spring has a lot of character due to its roar, steam, strong sulfurous smell, and surging wave action

Mud Volcano

- temperature: 184°F
- depth: 17 feet
- strongly acidic
- historically eruptive; now roils constantly

Kelly Warm Springs, Grand Teton National Park

Despite its proximity to the thousands of geothermal features of Yellowstone, Kelly Warm Springs is one of the only thermal springs within Jackson Hole. It has a year-round temperature of about 70°F, which makes it an ideal habitat for creatures that wouldn't ordinarily survive in this northern ecosystem. The fish and frog species depicted below represent several of the exotics that can be found in this unique spring. After the Kelly Flood of 1927, the spring produced more water than before, and, according to geologist J.David Love, as much as 5 million gallons per day now flow from the spring's source. The water within Kelly Warm Springs never freezes and so provides year-round habitat for waterfowl and fish-hunting birds such as kingfishers and eagles. The ground surrounding the springs is also warmer, which means that seasonal changes occur differently here. Snowpack melts earlier, wildflowers bloom earlier, ground squirrels emerge sooner from their deep hibernation, and insects such as butterflies can be found here as adults before most other places in the region.

American Bullfrog
Lithobates catesbeianus

Convict Cichlid
Cichlasoma nigrofasciatum
• native to Central America

Goldfish
Carassius auratus
• native to East Asia

Green Swordtail
Xiphophorus hellerii
• native to Central America

Yellowfin Goby
Acanthogobius flavimanus
• native to Asia

Guppy
Poecilia reticulata
• native to West Indies and South America

Speckled Dace
Rhinichthys osculus
• native to western U.S.

Waterfalls

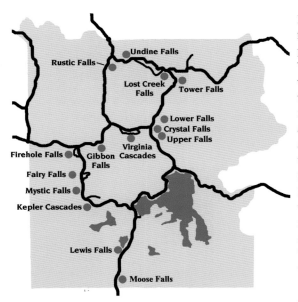

In addition to the flora, fauna, and geothermal phenomena of the Greater Yellowstone Ecosystem, waterfalls also enhance the beauty of this unique region. Yellowstone's falls are each distinct and there are hundreds of them scattered throughout the park. Many of them are in the backcountry; the southwest corner contains so many falls that it is known as "Cascade Corner." Grand Teton also has wonderful waterfalls, but aside from Hidden Falls few are as famous as such iconic landmarks as the Upper and Lower Falls of the Yellowstone River, Tower Falls, and Gibbon Falls. Two waterfalls, Upper and Lower Mesa Falls, are located outside of the parks but lie within the GYE and are charismatic enough to warrant inclusion here.

Moose Falls

- height: 30 feet
- located on Crawfish Creek and accessed by a very short hike just inside the South Gate

Lewis Falls

- height: 30 feet
- park on either side of Lewis River Bridge
- this falls and the river it is located on are both named after Meriwether Lewis despite the fact that the Lewis and Clark Expedition never traveled through Yellowstone

Kepler Cascades

- height: 100 to 150 feet
- named for Kepler Hoyt, 12-year-old son of territory govenor John Hoyt; they toured Yellowstone in 1881; roadside viewing platform

Mystic Falls

- height: 70 feet
- located on the Little Firehole River, this cascading waterfall is accessed by a 1-mile hike from the Biscuit Basin boardwalk

Fairy Falls

- height: 197 feet
- located on Fairy Creek and discovered by Ferdinand Hayden and J.W. Barlow in 1871

Firehole Falls

- height: 40 feet
- located on the Firehole River which derives its name from as early as the 1830s when trappers referred to valleys as "holes" and wildfires had burned a nearby valley

Gibbon Falls

- height: 84 feet
- located on the Gibbon River, named for General John Gibbon, who was recognized by members of the second Hayden survey for exploring the area

Virginia Cascade

- height: 60 feet
- located on the Gibbon River east of Norris and upstream of Gibbon Falls

Rustic Falls

- height: 47 feet
- located on Glen Creek, this waterfall was orginally labeled "West Gardner Falls" until being renamed in 1879 by park superintendent Philetus Norris

Undine Falls

- height: 60 feet
- located on Lava Creek, this falls is named for mythological creatures from German folklore known as Undines (pronounced *un-deens*), which were thought to inhabit areas around waterfalls

Lower Falls of the Yellowstone River

- height: 308 feet
- started forming about 48,000 years ago
- water passing through a notch in the upper-left lip of the falls creates a green streak before breaking into spray
- look for osprey nests on the rhyolite cliffs
- considered by many to be one of the most scenic waterfalls in the world
- photographed and painted by millions of visitors including Thomas Moran and William Henry Jackson during the 1871 Hayden Expedition

Crystal Falls

- height: 129 feet
- located on Cascade Creek, this waterfall is visible from Uncle Tom's Trail downriver from the Upper Falls of the Yellowstone River

Upper Falls of the Yellowstone River

- height: 109 feet
- located 0.5 mile upstream of Lower Falls. Visible from Uncle Tom's Trailhead, or walk the short trail from the loop road to the brink

Lost Creek Falls
- height: 40 feet
- located on Lost Creek; accessible by a 0.3-mile hike from Roosevelt Lodge

Tower Fall
- height: 132 feet
- located on Tower Creek and named for the towering pillars nearby

Grand Teton Waterfalls and Mesa Falls

Wilderness Falls

- height: 250 feet
- located on the west side of Jackson Lake, this waterfall is very remote to view up close but can be seen from many locations on the east side of the lake including Colter Bay

Glacier Falls

- height: 50 feet
- located up Glacier Gulch to the west of the Lupine Meadow Trailhead

Broken Falls

- height: about 300 feet with multiple drops
- located west of Lupine Meadows (north of Glacier Falls)

Hidden Falls

- height: 200 feet
- located up Cascade Canyon, 1.2 miles west of Jenny Lake; accessed by hiking around the lake or taking the ferry across

Lower Mesa Falls

- height: 85 feet
- located on the Henry's Fork of the Snake River in the Bridger-Teton National Forest, this falls is just downstream of the larger Upper Mesa Falls

Upper Mesa Falls

- height: 114 feet
- an impressive falls easily accessed from viewpoints on Mesa Falls Scenic Byway northeast of Ashton, Idaho

Mushrooms

Organisms in this group fall within the Fungi Kingdom. Fungi do not produce their own food through chlorophyll as most plants do. Instead, they get food from surrounding soil or other decaying matter such as scat and rotting wood. The mushrooms described in this section are really more of a "fruit," with the rest of the organism (called the *mycelium*) living underground for up to hundreds of years. Most mushrooms thrive in moist habitats and are more abundant in years with higher precipitation. When conditions are favorable, the mycelium sends threads up through the soil that then sprout as mushrooms, which produce thousands of microscopic seed-like spores.

In 1982, one of the most respected North American mycologists, Kent McKnight, conducted a survey of the fungi of Yellowstone and Grand Teton National Parks. This survey identified 474 species, but it is certain that many more are present in the region.

Fungi boast many fascinating superlatives, including being the second-largest group of organisms on the planet (behind insects) with an estimated 1.5 million species classified. These known species likely represent less than 10 percent of all fungi species on the planet. At one time fungi were classified with plants, but it is now known through genetic analysis that fungi are actually more closely related to mammals than they are to plants. Yet most plant life depends on fungi: by breaking down organic material, fungi make nutrients more readily available in the soil. Also, most vascular plants host symbiotic fungi, known as *mycorrhizae*, that live in the plants' roots and supply essential nutrients.

Some mushrooms are poisonous, some nutritious and delicious, while others are benign but unpalatable. The descriptions below don't include edibility: *absolute certain identification* is necessary for safe consumption. Many poisonous mushrooms look just like edibile species. Eating the wrong mushroom can lead to liver and kidney failure and death. Unless you are a trained expert, it's not worth the risk. Particularly poisonous mushrooms are noted in the descriptions.

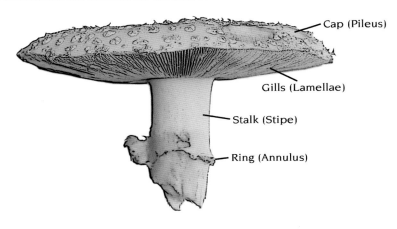

Cap (Pileus)

Gills (Lamellae)

Stalk (Stipe)

Ring (Annulus)

Fly Agaric
Amanitaceae Family
Amanita muscaria
- cap color can be white, yellow, or red with white "warts"
- poisonous

Russula
Russulaceae Family
Russula emetica
- red cap and very white gills and stalk
- poisonous (nicknamed the "sickener")

Russula
Russulaceae Family
Russula brunneola
- dark brown or gray cap with white gills and stalk
- often found in conifer forests

Rosy Russula
Russulaceae Family
Russula sanguinea
- cap and stalk reddish to light pink
- found in conifer forests

Soap Tricholoma
Tricholomataceae Family
Tricholoma saponaceum
- cap is typically gray or olive-colored but varies widely
- pink coloration at stalk's base (inside and out) is one of the best ways to identify
- found in conifer forests
- odor soap-like

Waxy Laccaria
Tricholomataceae Family
Laccaria laccata
- cap, stalk, and spores pink to light brown
- found in damp soil throughout spring, summer, and fall; one of the most common mushrooms in North America

Collybia
Tricholomataceae Family
Collybia spp.
- tough stalks that usually won't break when bent
- often found growing on the remains of other mushrooms

Oyster Mushroom
Tricholomataceae Family
Pleurotus pulmonarius
- white cap often lobed along edges
- gills extend relatively far down stalk
- commonly found on rotting logs

Shaggy Mane
Agaricaceae Family
Coprinus spp.
- light cap with dark scales underneath
- grows frequently from decomposing buried wood
- also known as "inky caps"

Psathyrella Mushroom
Psathyrellaceae Family
Psathyrella spp.
- gray cap and stalk (light brown when younger)
- often found within aspen forests or grassy meadows
- all parts very fragile

White Dunce Cap
Bolbitiaceae Family
Conocybe lactea

- long cap and narrow stalk, both white
- found in grassy areas including lawns

Cortinarius Mushroom
Cortinariaceae Family
Cortinarius spp.

- this genus has numerous species and varies greatly in appearance
- the presence of fine, web-like fibers within gills is the most distinct characteristic of this genus
- many of the species in this group are associated with the root systems of conifer trees (mycorrhizal)

Gold-pored Bolete
Boletaceae Family
Boletus spp.

- cap is brown to maroon with golden spores underneath
- found in conifer forests

Horse Mushroom
Agaricaceae Family
Agaricus arvensis

- light-colored with convex cap that is often centrally flattened
- stalk typically widens toward base
- found in open fields, frequently in groups

Slippery Jack
Suillaceae Family
Suillus tomentosus

- found within lodgepole pine forests
- caps are sticky to the touch and stalk typically has fine spots
- stains blue when handled

King Bolete
Boletaceae Family
Boletus edulis

- often very large
- found in conifer forests
- pores underneath cap vary from white to light yellow

Black-stemmed Leccinum
Boletaceae Family
Leccinum spp.

- orange to brown cap with white stalk usually flecked with black
- frequently found in aspen forests
- the genus *Leccinum* is fairly distinct but identification to species is often impossible in the field

Puffball
Lycoperdaceae Family
Lycoperdon perlatum

- cap has distinct spines when younger
- longer stem than most other puffballs gives appearance of an inverted pear

Puffball
Agaricaceae Family
Bovista spp.

- papery exterior covering dark spores
- often found in open meadows in association with cattle

Black Morel
Morchellaceae Family
Morchella elata

- dark, conical cap with vertical ridges
- hollow stalk lighter brown than cap
- common after forest fires

False Morel
Discinaceae Family
Gyromitra gigas

- orange, brain-like cap; grows lower to the ground than true morels
- poisonous

Plants

The Greater Yellowstone Ecosystem is home to more than 1,500 plant species. This field guide focuses on the more distinct and common species, organized primarily by family. If you find a plant that is similar to, but not exactly like, a species in this book, you are probably in the correct plant family, which is a good start in plant identification. Plants are infamous for having more than one common name, and even their Latin nomenclature can vary. This section gives the most frequently used names. Also, the first two pages of this section offer a quick look at wildflowers organized by color. For the more conspicuous plants, this can be a much simpler means of identification.

This field guide groups the plants of the GYE into trees, shrubs (including cattails and horsetails), and wildflowers. The distinction between trees and shrubs can be somewhat vague. For our purposes, both are woody plants but shrubs are less than 30 feet tall.

When encountering an unknown plant, look for as many details as possible. Notice where it is growing; the shape of leaves or needles; color, number, and shape of petals and sepals on flowers; whether the leaves are op-posite or alternate; and the presence of berries, cones, or fruit. Take ample field notes, or preserve a "speci-men" for later identification with a photograph or sketch of the plant. Please remember that it is illegal to pick flowers and plants in all national parks.

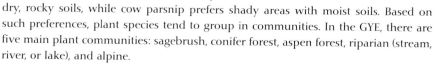

Plants are evolved to grow in certain habitats, determined primarily by a combination of soil type, moisture content of the soil, elevation, and aspect. Arrow–leaf balsamroot, for example, thrives on dry, rocky soils, while cow parsnip prefers shady areas with moist soils. Based on such preferences, plant species tend to group in communities. In the GYE, there are five main plant communities: sagebrush, conifer forest, aspen forest, riparian (stream, river, or lake), and alpine.

Plants rely on a variety of strategies for reproduction. The success of each species is completely dependent upon effective fertilization and dispersal. The majority of plants are either angiosperms (seeds contained in a fruit) or gymnosperms (seeds are "naked"). Conifers such as pine trees are a quintessential gymnosperm. The smaller male cones release millions of pollen grains that are carried on the wind and caught in resinous, sticky female cones, which are much larger and scaled. The fertilized seeds later drop out of the cone and are dispersed by squirrels and birds. Angiosperms comprise the flowering plants and rely on a variety of ways to transfer pollen, including wind, water, birds, bats, and insects. Flowers are frequently structured and scented in a particular way to invite specific pollinators to visit and ultimately deliver pollen to another plant. Species that are wind–pollinated tend to be much less showy, with smaller, more discrete flowers. In angiosperms, the fertilized seeds develop within a fruit. The fruit, in turn, may be dispersed by wind, water, or animals.

Flower Identification by Color

Page 66 Page 62 Page 76 Page 75 Page 72 Page 66

Page 81 Page 62 Page 78 Page 70 Page 76 Page 80

Page 72 Page 81 Page 79 Page 65 Page 81 Page 66

Page 69 Page 67 Page 70 Page 78 Page 78 Page 72

Page 73 Page 66 Page 73 Page 72 Page 74 Page 69

Page 79 Page 71 Page 63 Page 76 Page 74 Page 77

Page 71 Page 78 Page 67 Page 80 Page 73 Page 73

Page 71 Page 74 Page 70 Page 74 Page 61 Page 67

Page 67 Page 81 Page 76 Page 78 Page 74 Page 69

Page 63 Page 79 Page 69 Page 79 Page 77 Page 77

Page 79 Page 78 Page 71 Page 73 Page 75 Page 74

Page 75 Page 67 Page 77 Page 77 Page 75 Page 69

Page 67 Page 75 Page 68 Page 76 Page 73 Page 61

Page 73 Page 68 Page 69 Page 79 Page 68 Page 70

Page 80 Page 68 Page 79 Page 80 Page 72 Page 80

Page 66 Page 81 Page 70 Page 66 Page 68 Page 73

Page 81 Page 78 Page 80 Page 78 Page 70 Page 75

Page 68 Page 70 Page 76 Page 77

Conifer (Pinaceae) Family

This group consists of trees with evergreen needles. Identification within this group can be based on the number of needles within bunches and the characteristics and size of cones. Lodgepole pine is the most common conifer in the GYE.

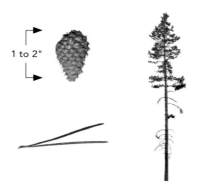

Lodgepole Pine
Pinus contorta

- height: 60 to 80 feet
- needles in packets of two
- grows moderately tall but very straight; slow growing
- cones are short and many are serotinous (seeds are sealed in resinous cones, which melt and release seeds in the high temperatures of a wildfire)
- re-seeds extensively after wildfires; young lodgepole pines are repopulating old burns throughout Yellowstone

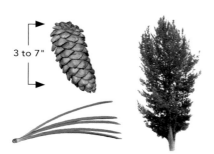

Limber Pine
Pinus flexilis

- height: 12 to 45 feet
- needles in packets of five
- name originates from twigs being more flexible than on other pines
- generally found at higher elevations than lodgepole pines but lower than whitebark pines (mixed pine forests are common)

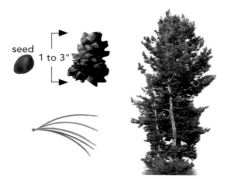

Whitebark Pine
Pinus albicaulis

- height: 30 to 50 feet
- needles in packets of five
- cones resemble limber pine but are shorter
- found at high elevations near treeline
- mountain pine beetles have killed entire forests of whitebark pine within the GYE
- seeds are highly nutritious; two species depend on them in particular: Clark's nutcracker, which is largely responsible for seed dispersal, and grizzly bears, which tend to favor whitebark seeds over other foods when available

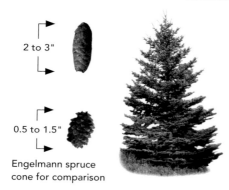

2 to 3"

0.5 to 1.5"

Engelmann spruce
cone for comparison

Colorado Blue Spruce
Picea pungens

- height: 75 to 110 feet
- spruce needles are singular; sharper to the touch than fir needles
- both blue and Engelmann spruce prefer moist habitats and can be found mixed with cottonwoods along rivers
- cone is noticeably smaller in Engelmann spruce
- blue spruce is commonly used for landscaping

Spruce aphid gall
(often mistaken for cone)

3"

Douglas-Fir
Pseudotsuga menziesii

- height: 70 to 110 feet
- needles singular, soft, and flat in cross section
- cones are distinct with three-pronged bracts protruding throughout
- not a "true fir" like subalpine fir, but a very popular Christmas tree
- one of GYE's largest trees in height and diameter; they grow much bigger in the moist Pacific Northwest

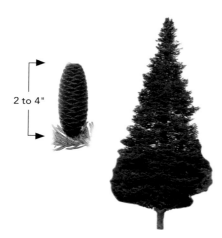

2 to 4"

Subalpine Fir
Abies lasiocarpa

- height: 60 to 100 feet
- singular needles, slightly longer than Douglas-fir needles
- cones are purple, grow upright on the highest branches, and drop the scales leaving a vertical stalk behind
- bark is smooth and gray (unlike any other conifer in GYE)
- subalpine firs occur up to treeline; stunted and twisted at high elevations

Willow (Salicaceae) Family

This family includes both trees and shrubs; all have flowers in tight clusters called catkins. Seeds are dispersed by wind in cotton-like tufts. The two species of willow shrubs represented below are common, but many species are present in the GYE and can be challenging to distinguish.

Quaking Aspen
Populus tremuloides
- height: 30 to 90 feet
- common throughout the Rocky Mountains
- leaves heart shaped; distinct white bark with dark scars throughout
- aspens primarily reproduce by cloning; an entire forest can be genetically identical and connected through its root system
- leaves turn intense golden in late September/early October

Narrowleaf Cottonwood
Populus angustifolia
- height: 20 to 90 feet
- leaves are elongated and pointed
- bark is gray and furrowed
- cottonwoods prefer moist areas near lakes and rivers
- state tree of Wyoming is plains cottonwood, which resembles this species
- in early summer, cottony seed tufts float through the air in great abundance

Booth's Willow
Salix boothii
- height: 6 to 9 feet
- leaves alternate in all willow species, often finely toothed
- like most willow species, found in riparian habitats

Narrowleaf Willow
Salix exigua
- height: 6 to 14 feet
- leaves long and narrow, often pale green and finely toothed

Rose (Rosaceae) Family

Characteristics of the shrubs in this family include five-petal flowers and alternate leaves. This family includes many commercially important plants such as roses, cherries, and apples.

Serviceberry
Amelanchier alnifolia

- height: 3 to 15 feet
- white five-petal flowers bloom in early summer
- berries are edible and favored by wildlife in fall

Wild Rose
Rosa woodsii

- height: 1 to 5 feet
- large five-petal flowers are typically pink
- fruits consist of bright red "rose hips," which are edible but not delicious

Chokecherry
Prunus virginiana

- height: 5 to 25 feet
- white five-petal flowers are arranged like a drooping bottlebrush
- berries hang in bunches and are edible to both people and wildlife (but taste better after a frost)

Shrubby Cinquefoil
Dasiphora fruticosa

- height: 10 to 50 inches
- bright yellow five-petal flowers
- commonly used in landscaping
- often found in open, dry areas
- not frequently browsed by wildlife

Bitterbrush
Purshia tridentata

- height: 20 to 40 inches
- small three-tipped leaves remain on plant year-round and become a critical food source for many ungulates during winter
- small light-yellow flowers seen in early summer

Black Hawthorn
Crataegus douglasii

- height: 3 to 14 feet
- small white five-petal flowers
- leaves are serrated and alternate

Birch-leaved Spiraea
Spiraea betulifolia

- height: 16 to 35 inches
- woody stem, flowers white and very small
- leaves are alternate and toothed toward tip
- a favored browse for grouse and deer

Thimbleberry
Rubus parviflorus

- height: 2 to 6 feet
- large leaves (4 to 8 inches wide) resemble maple leaves
- white five-petal flowers, 1 to 2 inches wide
- red berries are edible and favored by both people and wildlife

Western Mountain Ash
Sorbus scopulina

- height: 3 to 12 feet
- long serrated leaves
- bright red berries are densely bunched; though bitter, they attract several species of birds, notably waxwings

Cedar (Cupressaceae) Family

Family characteristics include evergreen leaves that are scale-like or needles. Fruits are blue and resemble berries.

Common Juniper
Juniperus communis

- height: 10 to 40 inches
- low to ground, spreading outward
- pointed needles in groups of three
- only circumpolar conifer across northern hemisphere

Rocky Mountain Juniper
Juniperus scopulorum

- height: 3 to 30 feet
- leaves with scales (not needles)
- more tree-like than common juniper
- male and female cones found on separate trees

Heath (Ericaceae) Family

Characteristics vary widely within this family, but leaves are often alternate; several species produce conspicuous berries.

Common Bearberry
Arctostaphylos uva-ursi

- height: 4 to 8 inches
- grows in mats low to the ground
- leaves alternate; bright red berries eaten readily by wildlife (including bears)
- also known as kinnikinnick

Prince's Pine
Chimaphila umbellata

- height: 4 to 12 inches
- pink flowers and serrated leaves are both slightly waxy
- prefers conifer forests
- also known as pipsissewa or wintergreen

Huckleberry
Vaccinium spp.

- height: 1 to 4 feet
- flowers resemble bearberry but berries are dark blue
- edible berries favored by people and wildlife

Grouse Whortleberry
Vaccinium scoparium

- height: 4 to 8 inches
- small pink flowers with bright red berries
- leaves alternate and finely serrated
- common in conifer forests and, as its name suggests, a favorite food of grouse

Miscellaneous Shrubs

Mountain Alder
Birch Family
Alnus incana

- height: 4 to 12 feet
- leaves are distinctly toothed
- flowers are tight catkins that develop into small cone-like structures
- usually found in riparian habitats

Tobaccobrush (Snowbrush)
Buckthorn Family
Ceanothus velutinus

- height: 1 to 4 feet
- small five-petal flowers
- leaves alternate, large (1 to 3 inches long), and waxy
- common pioneer after wildfires; seeds remain viable in the soil for long periods

Wyoming Big Sagebrush
Daisy Family
Artemisia tridentata

- height: 2 to 6 feet
- leaves evergreen, three lobed, and velvety
- extremely common in GYE on valley floors and low-elevation ridges
- successful due to its ability to thrive in relatively low-moisture soil and its toxicity to wildlife and livestock
- wind pollinated (unlike most species within the daisy family); its light yellow flowers, which bloom in late summer, don't need the showy charisma of typical insect-pollinated plants

Rabbitbrush
Daisy Family
Chrysothamnus spp.

- height: 1 to 3 feet
- narrow, alternate leaves (1 to 2 inches long)
- small yellow flowers bloom in late summer (much brighter than sagebrush flowers)
- several similar species of rabbitbrush can be found in GYE (all typically within sagebrush habitat)

Snowberry
Honeysuckle Family
Symphoricarpos oreophilus

- height: 30 to 40 inches
- leaves opposite and oval shaped
- flowers white or pink and tubular
- white berries are inedible

American Dwarf Mistletoe
Mistletoe Family
Arceuthobium americanum

- height: 4 to 12 feet
- parasitic (most common on lodgepole pines)

Northern Gooseberry
Currant Family
Ribes oxyacanthoides

- height: 12 to 40 inches
- leaves lobed, resembling maple leaves
- red berries are edible in both these species, but squaw currant berries are less palatable

Squaw Currant *(Ribes cereum)* for comparison

Rocky Mountain Maple
Maple Family
Acer glabrum

- height: 10 to 30 feet (could be classified as a shrub or small tree)
- leaves opposite and strongly toothed
- seeds enclosed in papery "wings"

Oregon Grape
Barberry Family
Mahonia repens

- height: 4 to 12 inches
- leaves alternate, marginally toothed, and waxy
- flowers densely clustered, bloom in early summer
- berries edible but unpalatable

Red-osier Dogwood
Dogwood Family
Cornus sericea

- height: 2 to 5 feet
- leaves opposite and distinctly veined
- berries are light colored, edible but sour

Buffaloberry
Oleaster Family
Shepherdia canadensis

- height: 2 to 5 feet
- leaves opposite and elliptical
- flowers subtle (found under leaves)
- bright red berries have a slippery texture and bitter taste

Cattails & Horsetails

Broadleaf Cattail
Cattail Family
Typha latifolia

- height: 3 to 8 feet
- leaves long and alternate
- thick dark brown female flowers below more subtle male flowers
- found in marshes and other wet areas

Scouring-rush
Horsetail Family
Equisetum hyemale

- height: 1 to 3 feet
- stems segmented and hollow
- stem terminates in cone-like spore cluster
- found in moist habitats

Lily (Liliaceae) Family

Characteristics of the lily family include parallel venation within the leaves and petals in threes or factor of threes.

Glacier Lily
Erythronium grandiflorum

- height: 2 to 8 inches
- each flower has two large basal leaves (close to ground)
- bright yellow flower has six petals; blooms in early summer at lower elevations
- edible roots favored by bears and rodents

Yellowbells
Fritillaria pudica

- height: 12 to 24 inches
- long, relatively thick leaves
- six-petal yellow flowers bloom in early summer
- strongly scented to attract pollinators
- roots and leaves are eaten by rodents, bears, deer, and elk

Sego Lily
Calochortus nuttallii

- height: 4 to 12 inches
- white three-petal flower with purple and yellow coloration toward base
- Utah state flower

Leopard Lily
Fritillaria atropurpurea

- height: 8 to 14 inches
- inconspicuous brown-purple flower
- blooms in early summer

Beargrass
Xerophyllum tenax

- height: 19 to 60 inches
- small white six-petal flowers in cluster; blooms every 2 to 9 years in early summer
- prefers dry soils on open slopes
- leaves are an important food source to bears
- Uncommon in the GYE; occurs along southern boundary of Yellowstone National Park

False Solomon's-seal
Maianthemum racemosum

- height: 6 to 24 inches
- leaves alternate
- small star-shaped, six-petal flowers densely clustered

Iris (Iridaceae) Family

Members of the iris family are monocots similar to lilies, but leaves are sharply edged and flowers have three stamens (six is more common in other similar families).

Western Blue Flag
Iris missouriensis

- height: 8 to 20 inches
- long, narrow, sword-like leaves
- flowers are usually pale blue with three petals that drape backward and three sepals
- blooms in early summer
- also called Rocky Mountain iris

Mountain Blue-eyed Grass
Sisyrinchium montanum

- height: 4 to 20 inches
- leaves found low and resemble grass
- flowers are purple with six pointed petals and yellow center
- distinctive flat, sharp-edged stem

Orchid (Orchidaceae) Family

Orchids are monocots with parallel-veined leaves, flower parts in threes, and flowers that are bilaterally symmetrical (equal vertically but not horizontally).

Fairyslipper
Calypso bulbosa

- height: 2 to 8 inches
- leaves are low to the ground and elliptical
- flower is a striking combination of pink, purple, and yellow with large lower "lip"
- found in conifer forests

Spotted Coralroot
Corallorhiza maculata

- height: 8 to 20 inches
- no green parts due to an absence of chlorophyll
- flowers are purple and spotted with a broader "lip" below
- associated with fungi, coralroots break down decaying matter within soil

White Bog Orchid
Platanthera dilatata

- height: 6 to 30 inches
- leaves alternate and wrap around stem
- flowers white, irregularly shaped, and fragrant
- found in open and moist habitats

Primrose Family

Shootingstar
Dodecatheon pulchellum

- height: 4 to 14 inches
- leaves elliptical and near ground (basal)
- flowers are vivid pink to purple with five inverted petals and yellow center
- found up to alpine regions, usually in moist habitats

Sunflower (Asteraceae) Family

This is the largest plant family in North America with over 20,000 individual species worldwide. Flowers are often made up of both outer (ray) and inner (disk) flowers. Several species in this family are exotics including tansy, bull thistle, knapweed, and dandelion.

Arrowleaf Balsamroot
Balsamorhiza sagittata

- height: 8 to 28 inches
- large leaves in the shape of an arrow, soft in texture
- often grows in bunches within sagebrush habitat and blooms earlier than mules-ears

Mules-ears
Wyethia amplexicaulis

- height: 12 to 24 inches
- similar to balsamroot but leaves are more elliptical and somewhat leathery
- also similar to sunflowers but has alternate leaves
- found in open sagebrush habitats

Heartleaf Arnica
Arnica cordifolia

- height: 8 to 28 inches
- leaves are opposite, toothed, soft, and heart shaped
- yellow ray flowers are more pointed and fewer than many other daisy species

Canada Goldenrod
Solidago canadensis

- height: 12 to 48 inches
- leaves narrow and alternate
- small flowers densely clustered

Common Tansy
Tanacetum vulgare

- height: 16 to 40 inches
- leaves alternate and deeply serrated
- small flowers with a central depression
- native to Europe but introduced across North America

Orange Agoseris
Agoseris aurantiaca

- height: 6 to 24 inches
- leaves are basal and narrow
- one of the only examples of an orange flower within the sunflower family
- stems are tall and seep a milky liquid when broken

Prairie Coneflower
Ratibida columnifera

- height: 3 to 4 feet
- leaves are elliptical and clasp stem
- unlike other daisies, coneflowers have either no ray flowers or just a few draping downward

Engelmann's Aster
Aster engelmannii

- height: 2 to 3 feet
- leaves alternate, elliptical, and (unlike other species in this genus) do not clasp stem
- ray flowers are more sparse than many other daisies

Showy Fleabane
Erigeron speciosus

- height: 10 to 20 inches
- leaves alternate, broad, and clasp the stem
- asters and fleabanes can be difficult to distinguish Fleabanes often flower earlier and have bracts beneath the flower organized into a single row; aster bracts are more chaotically arranged

Yellow Salsify
Tragopogon dubius

- height: 12 to 40 inches
- leaves alternate, narrow, and clasp stem
- bracts beneath ray flowers extend beyond the rest of the flower
- seedheads resemble dandelions, but larger

Yarrow
Achillea millefolium

- height: 4 to 26 inches
- leaves alternate, finely divided, and very fragrant
- ray flowers are usually white with light yellow disk flowers in the center
- yarrow is widely distributed across North America and has been used for a wide range of medicinal purposes

Musk Thistle
Carduus nutans

- height: up to 7 feet
- leaves spiny and alternate
- purple flowers densely packed containing thousands of seeds
- this is one of the most problematic invasive species (native to Europe and Asia) and can completely overtake an area when not controlled

Western Groundsel
Senecio spp.

- height: 1 to 3 feet
- several species of groundsels occur in GYE
- leaves of groundsels are more numerous than similar species, alternate, and serrated
- general flower characteristics include flowerhead bracts in one linear row and sparsely arranged ray flowers
- western groundsel is taller and more robust than most other groundsels

Common Dandelion
Taraxacum officinale

- height: 2 to 16 inches
- leaves basal and deeply notched into triangular lobes (largest lobe at tip)
- introduced species from Europe but a less common native species (horned dandelion) has leaves with less distinct lobes
- all parts of dandelions are edible

Slender-tipped Hawksbeard
Crepis acuminata

- height: 30 to 40 inches
- leaves alternate and clasping stem
- small yellow flowers comprised entirely of ray flowers (no disk flowers)

Oxeye Daisy
Chrysanthemum leucanthemum

- height: 8 to 30 inches
- leaves alternate and slightly lobed
- white ray flowers with yellow disk flowers
- a noxious invader from Europe

Common Sunflower
Helianthus annuus

- height: 4 to 16 inches
- leaves elliptical; may be opposite or alternate
- disk flowers dark colored

Spotted Knapweed
Centaurea maculosa

- height: 1 to 4 feet
- leaves alternate, blue-gray, and spiny
- flowers purple and consisting of disk flowers only
- introduced from Asia; one of the most problematic invasive species to control

Pussytoes
Antennaria spp.

- height: 4 to 10 inches
- leaves typically basal and narrow
- flowers typically white and consisting of ray flowers only
- often reproduces without pollination so that offspring are genetically identical to parents

Purslane (Portulacaceae) Family

Many species in this family have flowers with five petals
and are most distinct in having only two sepals.

Springbeauty
Claytonia lanceolata

- height: 2 to 7 inches
- leaves opposite and lance shaped
- pink flowers with five petals and two sepals
- entire plant is edible and favored by bears when blooming in early summer

Bitterroot
Lewisia rediviva

- height: 1 to 4 inches
- leaves basal and round
- flowers pink and multi-petaled (bloom in early summer)
- Montana state flower

Flax Family

Blue Flax
Linum lewisii

- height: 4 to 28 inches
- leaves alternate, small, tightly bound to stem
- flowers consist of five bright blue petals easily dislodged from plant

Stonecrop Family

Lance-leaved Stonecrop
Sedum lanceolatum

- height: 2 to 8 inches
- leaves alternate, fleshy, and lance tipped
- flowers are yellow and star shaped
- found at all elevations up to alpine

Geranium Family

Sticky Geranium
Geranium viscosissimum

- height: 15 to 35 inches
- leaves alternate, large, and deeply lobed
- pink flowers with five petals veined dark purple
- stems and leaves have fine hairs with sticky texture; can trap and dissolve insects for protein

Carrot (Apiaceae) Family

Species within the carrot family have alternate leaves that are fragrant and divided. Flowers are densely clustered into umbrella-like "umbels."

Water Hemlock
Cicuta douglasii

- height: 18 to 40 inches
- leaves alternate and divided
- white or light-green flowers in umbels, bloom midsummer
- very poisonous, often found in wet habitats

Yampah
Perideridia gairdneri

- height: 16 to 45 inches
- leaves alternate and very narrow
- small white flowers in umbels
- edible but similar in appearance to other poisonous carrot species

Cow Parsnip
Heracleum maximum

- height: 3 to 7 feet (overall large size is distinctive to this species)
- leaves alternate, very large, and deeply lobed
- white flowers are small with five petals forming collections of umbels that can be 12 inches across
- often found in moist habitats

Desert Parsley
Lomatium ambiguum

- height varies widely within Lomatium species (from low-lying wildflower to shrub-like plant)
- leaves divided and often fern-like (always fragrant)
- small yellow or white flowers in umbels

Sweet-cicely
Osmorhiza occidentalis

- height: 4 to 14 inches (long stemmed)
- leaves divided and toothed with fine hairs
- subtle flowers are typically light green; develop into seeds with barbs pointing upward
- often found in moist habitats

Pink (Caryophyllaceae) Family

Characteristics of the pink family include small, opposite
leaves and white or pink flowers with five petals.

Ballhead Sandwort
Arenaria congesta

- height: 2 to 12 inches
- leaves narrow and mostly basal
- flowers with five white petals
- long stemmed

Field Chickweed
Cerastium arvense

- height: 2 to 12 inches
- leaves opposite with fine hairs
- flowers with five white, lobed petals

Moss Campion
Silene acaulis

- height: 1 to 3 inches
- spreads widely into moss-like cushions
- pink flowers with five petals
- found in alpine habitats

Bellflower Family

Harebell
Campanula rotundifolia

- height: 2 to 8 inches
- stem leaves opposite and narrow; basal leaves are more rounded
- light blue flowers have five petals and can be singular or multiple on each plant

Cactus Family

Prickly-pear Cactus
Opuntia polyacantha

- height: 4 to 20 inches
- leaves consist of protective spines
- flower petals yellow and overlapping

Bleeding Heart Family

Flowers within this family have two distinctly asymmetrical pairs of petals.

Steer's Head
Dicentra uniflora

- height: 1 to 2 inches
- unusual flowers resemble a cow's horns and skull
- blooms early in dry habitats
- poisonous

Golden Corydalis
Corydalis spp.

- height: 4 to 12 inches
- leaves alternate and divided
- poisonous

Evening Primrose Family

Four petals and four (often brightly colored) sepals are characteristic of this family.

Fireweed
Chamerion angustifolium

- height: 1 to 6 feet
- leaves alternate and fading to red by fall
- pink flowers with four broad petals
- blooms in late summer; common after wildfires

Evening Primrose
Oenothera cespitosa

- height: 2 to 4 inches (very low-lying)
- heart-shaped petals are white or light pink
- bloom at night and pollinated by moths

Pea (Fabaceae) Family

Pea species have seed pods and flowers with banners, wings, and a keel.

Lupine
Lupinus spp.

- height: 5 to 40 inches
- several species of lupine occur within the GYE; all have blue or purple flowers with structures typical of the pea family
- leaves of lupine are divided into 8 to 10 narrow leaflets

Red Clover
Trifolium pratense

- height: 8 to 30 inches
- leaves alternate and divided into three elliptical leaflets
- flowers deep rose to nearly white
- native to Europe but widespread across North America

American Vetch
Vicia americana

- height: 1 to 4 feet
- leaves alternate and pinnate
- flower varies from purple to blue
- stems are square and climbing

Pulse Milkvetch
Astragalus miser

- height: 8 to 25 inches
- leaves alternate and divided into multiple elliptical leaflets
- flowers white with purple tips

Buttercup (Ranunculaceae) Family

Flower structure within this family varies widely and includes species such as buttercups, which are radially symmetrical, as well as species with spurred petals such as larkspur and columbine. Several species have showy sepals rather than petals.

Monkshood
Aconitum columbianum

- height: 2 to 7 feet
- leaves alternate and divided into large lobes
- dark purple flowers have large hood above and two winged petals below
- found in moist habitats
- very poisonous

Rocky Mountain Columbine
Aquilegia coerulea

- height: 8 to 26 inches
- basal leaves are large and three lobed; stem leaves are similar but smaller and more sparse
- flower varies from white to light blue with unique spurs protruding backward
- typically pollinated by hummingbirds or sphinx moths

Larkspur
Delphinium spp.

- height: 5 to 40 inches
- several species of larkspur occur in the GYE and vary in height and leaf structure
- all species have dark purple flowers with a specialized upper sepal that projects backward in a distinct spur
- poisonous to livestock and people

Sagebrush Buttercup
Ranunculus glaberrimus

- height: 4 to 8 inches
- leaves basal and elliptical
- yellow flowers have five petals and five sepals
- one of the GYE's earliest blooming wildflowers
- found in open sagebrush habitats

Hairy Clematis
Clematis hirsutissima

- height: 3 to 8 inches
- leaves are soft and divided multiple times into narrow segments
- four dark blue or purple sepals resemble petals
- also known as sugarbowl

Blue Clematis
Clematis occidentalis

- length: 2 to 6 feet
- leaves opposite and divided into three leaflets on stems
- light-blue flowers have four sepals that resemble petals
- climbing vine, often on shrubs

Pasqueflower
Anemone patens

- height: 4 to 16 inches
- leaves finely divided
- flowers comprised of five to seven blue or white sepals with no petals visible
- poisonous to eat and irritating to the skin

Marsh Marigold
Caltha leptosepala

- height: 4 to 16 inches
- leaves are thick and sometimes found only at base of plant
- white sepals (not petals) surround yellow-centered flower
- blooms early and in saturated soils

Globeflower
Trollius laxus

- height: 4 to 18 inches
- leaves alternate and deeply lobed
- flower white to light yellow with five to nine petal-like sepals
- prefers moist habitats
- poisonous

Baneberry
Actaea rubra

- height: 12 to 40 inches
- leaves alternate, divided into threes, and toothed
- small white flowers in dense clusters
- entire plant (including berries) very poisonous

Meadow Buttercup
Ranunculus spp.

- height: 10 to 25 inches
- most leaves basal, alternate, and divided into threes; smaller leaves may be found along stem
- bright yellow flowers comprised of five petals
- introduced from Europe
- can be a skin irritant

Western Meadowrue
Thalictrum occidentale

- height: 12 to 40 inches
- leaves alternate, divided into threes, and tri-lobed
- purple or light green flowers are small and fragile
- male and female flowers are found on separate plants and can be distinguished by anther clusters drooping below the male flowers

Gentian (Gentianaceae) Family

Species in this family typically have four to five united petals, stamens fused to the petal wall, and opposite leaves.

Green Gentian
Frasera speciosa

- height: 1 to 6 feet
- leaves long (10 to 20 inches) and basal first year (doesn't flower its first year)
- light yellow or light green flowers have four petals and are numerous along tall, thick stem

Bog Gentian
Gentiana calycosa

- height: 2 to 12 inches
- leaves opposite, elliptical, and clasp one another around stem
- dark purple flower is fused at base
- found in moist habitats
- pleated gentian is similar but leaves are more distinctly fringed

Phlox (Polemoniaceae) Family

Flower and leaf structure vary greatly within this family. Flower parts are often in fives.

Scarlet Gilia
Ipomopsis aggregata

- height: 6 to 24 inches
- leaves alternate and divided into thin leaflets
- bright red flowers are tubular and star shaped
- hummingbirds pollinate gilia and are attracted to red coloration

Phlox
Phlox longifolia

- height: 1 to 4 inches
- phlox species are typically low to the ground but can be taller
- all phlox have opposite leaves and five white or pink petals

Borage (Boraginaceae) Family

Borage flowers have five sepals and five fused petals.

Bluebells
Mertensia spp.

- height: 4 to 20 inches
- leaves elliptical and alternate
- blue flowers often in clusters
- flower shape is similar within different bluebell species, but height and leaf shape vary

Mountain Forget-me-not
Myosotis spp.

- height: 2 to 12 inches
- leaves alternate and narrow
- light blue flowers have yellow center and five lobes

Rose (Rosaceae) Family

Wildflowers in the rose family have alternate leaves and flowers with five petals.

White Cinquefoil
Potentilla arguta

- height: 12 to 40 inches
- leaves divided and toothed
- white flowers have five petals with yellow center
- most other cinquefoil species are similar in structure but have yellow flowers

Strawberry
Fragaria vesca

- height: 2 to 6 inches
- leaves divided into three leaflets
- fruits resemble store-bought strawberries but much smaller

Prairie Smoke
Geum triflorum

- height: 4 to 12 inches
- flowers pink and nodding
- also called old man's whiskers

Buckwheat Family

Sulphur Buckwheat
Eriogonum umbellatum

- height: 2 to 15 inches
- leaves mostly basal and elliptical
- white, light yellow, or pink flowers in tight umbels resembling flowers of the carrot family
- many species of similarly structured buckwheat occur in the GYE; all tend to prefer dry, open habitats

Mint Family

Horsemint
Agastache urticifolia

- height: 16 to 50 inches
- leaves are opposite, coarsely toothed, and smell strongly of mint
- purple flowers are densely clustered
- like other members of this family, horsemint has square stems

Violet Family

Violets usually have alternate leaves with asymmetrical flower parts in fives.

Canada Violet
Viola canadensis

- height: 4 to 16 inches
- leaves broad and heart shaped
- species within this genus have three lower petals and two upper petals that bend backward

Yellow Violet
Viola nuttallii

- height: 2 to 8 inches
- like Canada violet but with basal leaves and yellow flowers
- lower petal has dark purple streaks toward base

Figwort (Scrophulariaceae) Family

Figwort flowers (excluding paintbrush species) are uniquely structured with
two-lobed upper petals and three-lobed lower petals. Leaves often opposite.

Wyoming Paintbrush
Castilleja spp.

- height: 8 to 24 inches
- leaves alternate and lance shaped
- bright coloration is on bracts that obscure the true flower parts
- Wyoming state flower

Yellow Paintbrush
Castilleja occidentalis

- height: 4 to 18 inches
- similar to Wyoming paintbrush but with narrower leaves and yellow bracts

Sulphur Paintbrush
Castilleja sulphurea

- height: 4 to 18 inches
- similar to other paintbrush species but with white bracts
- most paintbrush species have no scent and bloom throughout summer

Pink Monkeyflower
Mimulus lewisii

- height: 12 to 30 inches
- leaves opposite and pointed
- purple flowers are typical figwort structure
- often found in moist habitats at higher elevations

Yellow Monkeyflower
Mimulus guttatus

- height: 4 to 20 inches
- similar in structure to pink monkeyflower but yellow flowers are spotted purple toward base of lower petals
- found in moist habitats at lower elevations, often in geyser basins

Blue Penstemon
Penstemon spp.

- height: 2 to 16 inches
- several species of penstemon are present in the GYE; most have blue flowers with typical figwort structure and opposite leaves
- most penstemons prefer dry, open habitats

Whipple's Penstemon
Penstemon whippleanus

- height: 4 to 12 inches
- similar to other penstemons, but flowers vary from pale pink to maroon and inside of lower petals is streaked dark purple

Elephanthead
Pedicularis groenlandica

- height: 8 to 32 inches
- leaves mostly basal and divided into toothed leaflets
- pink flowers resemble the head of an elephant with lower lobes as ears and upper lobes as the trunk
- found in wet habitats

Common Toadflax
Linaria vulgaris

- height: 8 to 24 inches
- leaves alternate and narrow
- yellow flowers with dark yellow or orange lower lip
- introduced from Europe and Asia
- also known as butter-and-eggs

Bracted Lousewort
Pedicularis bracteosa

- height: 10 to 24 inches
- leaves alternate and strongly resemble ferns
- yellow flowers bloom sparsely along spiked tips
- prefers moist habitats

Common Mullein
Verbascum thapsus

- height: 16 to 72 inches
- leaves alternate, broad, and very soft
- yellow flowers are five lobed and arranged in clusters along tall stem
- native to Europe and Asia; introduced across North America

Parrot's Beak
Pedicularis racemosa

- height: 8 to 20 inches
- leaves alternate and finely toothed
- white flowers with three-lobed lower lip

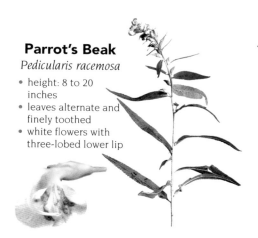

Yellow Owl's-clover
Orthocarpus luteus

- height: 4 to 16 inches
- leaves alternate and narrow
- yellow flowers arranged in clusters toward tip

Saxifrage (Saxifragaceae) Family

Saxifrage flowers are typically radially symmetrical with five petals and five sepals.

Fringed Grass-of-Parnassus
Parnassia fimbriata

- height: 4 to 12 inches
- leaves basal and heart shaped
- white, lacy flowers have five petals
- found in moist habitats

Small-flowered Woodland Star
Lithophragma parviflorum

- height: 4 to 12 inches
- basal leaves are divided multiple times
- white five-petal flowers significantly lobed and star-like
- prefers dry habitats

Mallow Family

Mountain Hollyhock
Iliamna rivularis

- height: 2 to 5 feet
- leaves alternate and resemble maple leaves
- pink flowers have five large petals

Madder Family

Northern Bedstraw
Galium boreale

- height: 8 to 22 inches
- narrow leaves extend from stem in whorls of four
- small white flowers in clusters

Mustard Family

Western Wallflower
Erysimum asperum

- height: 5 to 12 inches
- leaves alternate and grayish
- yellow flowers have four petals
- found in dry habitats

Water-lily Family

Yellow Water-lily
Nuphar lutea

- thick, heart-shaped leaves
- yellow flowers are cupped
- found floating in ponds

Grass (Poaceae) Family

It can be difficult to distinguish among the many grass species. Leaves are narrow with parallel veins. Flowers are inconspicuous and made up of spikelets at each tip.

Smooth Brome
Bromus inermis

- height: 1 to 3 feet
- non-native (often found along roads)
- flowers in single clusters and tips may be purplish

Timothy
Phleum spp.

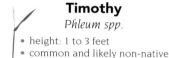

- height: 1 to 3 feet
- common and likely non-native
- named for early 1700s Maryland farmer Timothy Hanson

Kentucky Bluegrass
Poa pratensis

- height: 6 to 24 inches
- non-native
- tips of leaves are keel shaped
- most common lawn species in region

Idaho Fescue
Festuca idahoensis

- height: 2 to 6 inches
- leaves stiff and sharp
- common at higher elevations

Needlegrass
Stipa comata

- height: 1 to 2 feet
- tips are divided and tufted
- common in sagebrush habitats

Prairie Junegrass
Koeleria macrantha

- height: 8 to 20 inches
- less tightly bunched than Idaho fescue
- found in open, dry habitats

Reed Canarygrass
Phalaris arundinacea

- height: 2 to 3 feet
- leaf tips occasionally black
- flowers are light yellow in tight clusters
- favors moist habitats

Basin Wildrye
Elymus cinereus

- height: 3 to 8 feet
- leaves sharp-edged, broader than most grasses
- flowers (spikelets) overlapping and more two-dimensional than other grasses
- often found in isolated bunches

Slender Wheatgrass
Elymus trachycaulus

- height: 2 to 4 feet
- leaves with tiny hairs on upper surface
- spikelets tall and slightly overlapping

Crested Wheatgrass
Agropyron cristatum

- height: 2 to 3 feet
- leaves with tiny hairs on upper surface
- spikelets dense and in rows
- introduced from Asia and widespread across North America

Foxtail Barley
Hordeum jubatum

- height: 1 to 2 feet
- purple flower clusters arranged densely and nodding
- found in a variety of habitats, often along roadsides

Sedge
Family Cyperaceae
Carex spp.

- height: 4 to 20 inches
- prefers wet areas
- stems usually triangular, terminate in a short, dense spikelet

Insects

Lacking in both size and the immediate charisma of vertebrates, members of the insect class are easy to overlook and under-appreciate. They represent about 75 percent of animal life on Earth and can be found in virtually every environment, including the high temperatures of Yellowstone's geothermal features. The United States and Canada are home to almost 90,000 known species of insects and new species are still being discovered. Despite the fact that insects pose enormous problems as agricultural pests and as vectors for diseases, they are a critical part of any ecosystem in their roles as predators, prey, scavengers, and pollinators. Pollination by insects is vital to many wild and cultivated plants and provides a service worth billions of dollars.

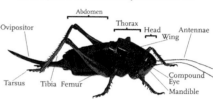

The basic anatomy of an insect consists of the head, thorax, and abdomen. Other features shared by most insects include three pairs of legs, one pair of antennae, two pairs of wings (some have just one pair and others are wingless), and compound or simple eyes. Another important part of an insect's structure is its exoskeleton (as opposed to the endoskeleton found in vertebrates), which is the durable armor that provides a protective framework, and also facilitates the exchange of water and gasses.

Accurate identification of insects can be challenging. Their small size makes observing individual characteristics difficult. Their sheer numbers mean that there are often hundreds of very similar species to discern from. And the various stages in their life cycles pose the problem that a single species will look strikingly different as an egg, larva, pupa, and, finally, as an adult. As with identifying plants, mushrooms, or birds, the best way to identify insects is to get to know group characteristics. Because there are so many, the best place to start is insect orders. There really aren't that many, and each one has certain unique characteristics. By recognizing that a "mystery" insect belongs in the fly order as opposed to the beetle order, you've just eliminated thousands of possibilities.

The following pages are organized by order, and each section begins with a very brief description of the qualities typical of that order. The notes associated with each image often apply to other insects within that individual's family. The size of each insect described and depicted here is an average, so bear in mind that sizes can vary. The images and descriptions for this section cover only a small percentage of the insects that make the GYE home, but they do represent many of the most commonly seen types and should help in narrowing down an unidentified insect.

The traditional means of learning about insects involves collecting, killing, and mounting them. This is prohibited in national parks, so a better alternative is to simply observe them in their natural state. For larger species such as dragonflies and butterflies, a pair of binoculars will provide amazing detail of their coloration and anatomy. For smaller insects, a good hand lens will draw you into the alien-like characteristics of many of these unique creatures.

Earwig (Dermaptera) Order

The long cerci (hind appendages) are distinct within this order.
Earwigs have four wings, relatively flattened bodies, and are brown.

Earwig
Forficula auricularia

- length: 0.5 to 0.75 inch
- large forceps
- native to Europe but widespread across North America
- despite name, are not known to crawl into people's ears

Lacewing, Fish Fly, & Antlion (Neuroptera) Order

Species in this order have four membranous, evenly sized wings
(with noticeable veins). Antennae are usually pronounced and segmented.

Fish Fly
Corydalidae Family
Sialis velata

- length: 0.25 to 0.75 inch
- wings distinctly veined and often folded in an inverted V above body

Brown Lacewing
Raphidiidae Family
Hemerobius pacificus

- length: 0.25 to 0.5 inch
- relatively large eyes
- mouthparts distinctly pointed

Mantidfly
Mantispidae Family
Climaciella brunnea

- length: 0.75 to 1 inch
- several characteristics resemble true mantids including predatory front legs and triangular head with large eyes

Green Lacewing
Chrysopidae Family
Chrysopa spp.

- length: up to 1 inch
- body usually green in color with copper eyes
- typically feed on aphids

Antlion
Myrmeleontidae Family
Myrmeleon spp.

- length: 1.25 to 1.5 inches
- larvae make funnel-shaped pits to trap prey

Antlion
Myrmeleontidae Family
Brachynemurus spp.

- length: 1 to 2 inches
- long bodied (extending beyond wing tips)

Grasshopper & Cricket (Orthoptera) Order

Members of this order are recognizable by their specialized hind legs for jumping. Most species have leathery forewings covering membranous hindwings.

Spur-throated Grasshopper
Acrididae Family
Melanoplus mexicanus

- length: 1.5 to 1.75 inches
- name originates from pronounced spur on ventral side between two front legs

Two-striped Mermiria
Acrididae Family
Mermiria bivittata

- length: 1 to 2 inches
- strongly angled face
- dark stripe extends from eye along side

Red-shanked Grasshopper
Acrididae Family
Xanthippus corallipes

- length: 1.5 to 2 inches
- wings banded
- back leg has three stripes on exterior and is dark red on interior
- body often dark spotted

Valley Grasshopper
Acrididae Family
Oedaleonotus borckii

- length: 0.5 to 0.75 inch
- this species is also spur throated like *Melanoplus* described above

Band-winged Grasshopper
Acrididae Family
Arphia frigida

- length: 1.25 to 1.5 inches
- distinct orange band on hindwing
- this group is commonly heard clicking in flight

Broad-banded Grasshopper
Acrididae Family
Trimerotropis latifasciata

- length: 1.25 to 1.5 inches
- hindwing banded (usually yellow and black)
- lower hind leg often red or orange

Clear-winged Grasshopper
Acrididae Family
Camnula pellucida

- length: 1 to 1.25 inches
- very similar to band-winged grasshopper but with clear hindwings

Pygmy Grasshopper
Tetrigidae Family
Tetrix subulata

- length: 0.25 to 0.5 inch
- often found near water

Jerusalem Cricket
Stenopelmatidae Family
Stenopelmatus spp.

- length: 1.25 to 2 inches
- no wings but long antennae

Camel Cricket
Rhaphidophoridae Family
Ceuthophilus spp.

- length: 1.25 to 2 inches
- wingless with very long antennae and long legs

Meadow Katydid
Tettigoniidae Family
Conocephalus fasciatus

- length: 1 to 1.25 inches
- green body and face

Mormon Cricket
Tettigoniidae Family
Anabrus simplex

- length: 1.5 to 2.25 inches
- adults long and stocky
- long antennae and dark "amored" plates
- females with extremely long ovipositor (sword-like appendage projecting from abdomen)

Tree Cricket
Gryllidae Family
Oceanthus spp.

- length: 0.25 to 0.5 inch
- long, narrow head
- mouth projects more forward than other species

Field Cricket
Gryllidae Family
Gryllus spp.

- length: 0.75 to 1.5 inches
- prominant spines on lower rear legs
- often dark in coloration

Beetle (Coleoptera) Order

This enormous group represents 40 percent of all insects and is the largest order in the animal kingdom (over 20,000 species in North America). Adults have tough forewings covering membranous hindwings, both meeting in a straight line down the back.

Big Sand Tiger Beetle
Carabidae Family
Cicindela formosa

- length: 0.5 to 0.75 inch
- brown or maroon with white markings

Predaceous Ground Beetle
Carabidae Family
Carabus spp.

- length: 0.75 to 1.25 inches
- dark or slightly metallic
- preys upon other insects

Metallic Ground Beetle
Carabidae Family
Chlaenius spp.

- length: 0.25 to 0.75 inch
- iridescent coloration
- often has fine hairs visible on head

Predaceous Water Beetle
Dytiscidae Family
Rhantus spp.

- length: 0.25 to 0.5 inch
- head often spotted or blotchy
- found in slow-moving or still water

Water Scavenger Beetle
Hydrophilidae Family
Hydrochara spp.

- length: 0.5 to 0.75 inch
- color varies from green to dark brown
- distinct spine on ventral side
- found in still water

Giant Water Scavenger Beetle
Hydrophilidae Family
Hydrophilus triangularis

- length: 1 to 1.5 inches
- large size is distinctive
- found in still water across North America

Carrion Beetle
Silphidae Family
Necrophila spp.

- length: 0.5 to 0.75 inch
- dark overall with lighter head or pronotum
- found on carrion or decaying fungus

Rove Beetle
Staphylinidae Family
Creophilus maxillosus

- length: 0.25 to 0.75 inch
- dark body with lighter horizontal bands
- found on carrion and scat

Cottonwood Stag Beetle
Lucanidae Family
Lucanus mazama

- length: 1 to 1.25 inches
- dark bodied with distinct pinching jaws

Metallic Wood-boring Beetle
Buprestidae Family
Buprestis spp.

- length: 0.5 to 0.75 inch
- green or brown, occasionally with yellow marking along back

Metallic Wood-boring Beetle
Buprestidae Family
Acmaeodera spp.

- length: 0.5 to 0.75 inch
- mottled yellow and black coloration
- often found within flowers

Click Beetle
Elateridae Family
Ctenicera spp.

- length: 0.25 to 0.5 inch
- name originates from clicking sound made when jumping
- adults often on flowers

Click Beetle
Elateridae Family
Ampedus spp.

- length: 0.25 to 0.5 inch
- similar to *Ctenicera* but wings may be more orange in color

Firefly
Lampyridae Family
Pyropyga spp.

- length: 0.25 to 0.5 inch
- dark overall with some red toward head
- smaller and with less-pronounced light organs than other firefly species

Soldier Beetle
Cantharidae Family
Chauliognathus spp.

- length: 0.5 to 0.75 inch
- patterned yellow and black
- often found in flowers

Carpet Beetle
Dermestidae Family
Dermestes spp.

- length: 0.25 to 0.5 inch
- dark body, often oval shaped
- antennae clubbed
- feed on carrion

Checkered Beetle
Cleridae Family
Enoclerus spp.

- length: 0.25 to 0.5 inch
- brightly colored red and black
- proportionally large head

Checkered Beetle
Cleridae Family
Trichodes spp.

- length: 0.25 to 0.5 inch
- like *Enoclerus* checkered beetle but with smaller head and more mottled coloration

European Dung Beetle
Scarabaeidae Family
Aphodius fimetarius

- length: 0.25 inch
- species in this group can be all brown or have red wings
- frequently found in cow dung

Flower Chafer Beetle
Scarabaeidae Family
Euphoria spp.

- length: 0.5 inch
- wide and flat bodied
- antennae clubbed
- feeds on flower nectar or pollen

Anteater Scarab Beetle
Scarabaeidae Family
Cremastocheilus spp.

- length: 0.25 to 0.5 inch
- dark colored and flattened
- preys upon ants

Hide Beetle
Trogidae Family
Trox spp.

- length: 0.25 to 0.5 inch
- dark colored with highly textured dorsal surface
- found in the hides of decomposing animals

June Beetle
Scarabaeidae Family
Diplotaxis spp

- length: 0.25 to 1 inches
- dark and shiny
- feeds on flowers and other plant material

Lined June Beetle
Scarabaeidae Family
Polyphylla spp.

- length: 1 to 1.25 inches
- large size and light-colored lines are distinctive

Snout Beetle
Curculionidae Family
Cryptorhynchus spp.

- length: up to 0.25 inch
- long beak
- antennae are both elbowed and clubbed

Thistle Weevil
Curculionidae Family
Cleonus spp.

- length: up to 0.25 inch
- similar beak and antennae as snout beetles, but lighter with dorsal stripes

Weevil
Curculionidae Family
Otiorhynchus spp.

- length: up to 0.25 inch
- antennae are both elbowed and clubbed
- squared head

Sap-feeding Beetle
Nitidulidae Family
Glischrochilus spp.

- length: up to 0.5 inch
- dark colored and may have irregular orange spots on wings

Ladybird Beetle
Coccinelidae Family
Hippodamia spp.

- length: 0.25 to 0.4 inch
- can be red or brown with black spots
- feeds on aphids

Ladybird Beetle
Coccinelidae Family
Coccinella spp.

- length: up to 0.25 inch
- usually fewer spots than *Hippodomia* ladybirds
- head often hidden

Two-spotted Ladybird Beetle
Coccinelidae Family
Adalia spp.

- length: up to 0.25 inch
- similar to other ladybirds but usually with just two black spots
- antennae clubbed

Desert Stink Beetle
Tenebrionidae Family
Eleodes spp.

- length: up to 1 inch
- dark colored and often seen with abdomen thrust upward
- emits unpleasant odor when bothered

Mountain Pine Beetle
Scolytidae Family
Dendroctonus ponderosae

- length: up to 0.25 inch
- this native beetle is responsible for the death of millions of lodgepole and whitebark pines throughout the GYE
- adults emerge in July and August leaving exit holes and consequent "pitch tubes" on the bark of infested trees

Darkling Ground Beetle
Tenebrionidae Family
Coniontis spp.

- length: up to 0.5 inch
- species in this group vary widely but usually have dark, flattened bodies
- found on the ground (often in decaying matter)

Blister Beetle
Meloidae Family
Lytta spp.

- length: 0.5 to 0.75 inch
- "beaded" antennae and orange or red head are characteristic of this group

Blister Beetle
Meloidae Family
Epicauta spp.

- length: 0.5 to 0.75 inch
- dark bodied with less "beaded" antennae than *Lytta* species
- name originates from chemical on exoskeleton capable of causing blistering on mammal's skin

Blister Beetle
Meloidae Family
Epicauta spp.

- length: 0.5 to 0.75 inch
- similar characteristics as the species described to the left, but with much paler and speckled body

Long-horned Beetle (Cerambycidae) Family

This very large family of beetles (about 1,000 in North America alone) varies widely in appearance, color, and markings. All have extremely long antennae and a somewhat cylindrical body shape. Often found in forested areas.

Banded Alder Borer
Rosalia spp.

- length: 1 to 1.25 inches
- three white stripes along back and single white dot on thorax

Cactus Long-horned Beetle
Moneilema spp.

- length: up to 1 inch
- antennae are checkered black and white

Flat-faced Long-horned Beetle
Monochamus spp.

- length: 1 to 1.25 inches
- extremely long antennae
- body color mottled black and gray

Long-horned Beetle
Prionus californicus

- length: 0.75 to 1.25 inches
- male's antennae more serrated than female's

Milkweed Long-horned Beetle
Tetraopes femoratus

- length: up to 0.5 inch
- red or orange bodies with black spots
- often associated with milkweed plants

Oak Borer
Enaphalodes spp.

- length: 1 to 1.25 inches
- extremely long segmented antennae

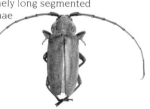

pronotum

Long-horned Beetle
Crossidius spp.

- length: 0.25 to 0.75 inch
- coloration may be brown, red, black, or yellow
- head vertical or angled slightly forward
- pronotum (see arrow on left species) often wider toward the middle

Long-horned Beetle
Batyle ignicoilis

- length: 0.25 to 0.5 inch
- often found on flowers

Flower Long-horned Beetle
Rhagium inquisitor

- length: 0.5 to 0.75 inch
- mottled coloration and broad "shoulders" are distinctive in this group

Flower Long-horned Beetle
Stenocorus nubifer

- length: 0.5 to 0.75 inch
- broad shouldered

Red-shouldered Pine Borer
Stictoleptura canadensis

- length: 0.5 to 0.75 inch
- similar to the other flower long-horns, but with clear black and red markings
- often found in conifer forests

Leaf Beetle (Chrysomelidae) Family

The species in this large family of beetles are often streaked yellow and black, with round or oval-shaped bodies. Antennae are relatively short. These beetles are found on flowers or leaves, often preferring a particular plant species.

Leaf Beetle
Calligrapha spp.

- length: 0.25 to 0.5 inch

Leaf Beetle
Leptinotarsa spp.

- length: 0.25 to 0.5 inch

Leaf Beetle
Chrysochus spp.

- length: 0.25 to 0.5 inch

Leaf Beetle
Trirhabda spp.

- length: 0.25 to 0.5 inch

Fly (Diptera) Order

Flies fill a wide variety of niches: food for many animals, pollinators, and parasites (some species are bloodsuckers). One important characteristic of this order is that flies have only one pair of membranous wings (most insect orders have two). Many fly species have pronounced compound eyes and mouthparts designed for sucking. Larvae are often aquatic.

Mosquito
Culicidae Family
Anopheles spp.

- length: 0.125 to 0.25 inch
- long probiscus, narrow body, and very long-legged
- lays eggs in still water

larva

Midge
Chironomidae Family

- length: 0.125 inch
- body and appendages have "feathery" appearance
- common in large swarms but non-biting

larva

Crane Fly
Tipulidae Family
Tipula spp.

- length: 1 to 1.25 inches (plus long legs)
- extremely long and fragile legs

March Fly
Bibionidae Family
Philia spinipes

- length: 0.25 inch
- dark bodies (often covered in fine hairs)
- short antennae

Robber Fly
Asilidae Family
Mallophora spp.

- length: up to 0.75 inch
- these robber flies mimic bees and strongly resemble them in flight

Hover Fly
Syrphidae Family
Arctophila spp.

- length: 0.25 to 0.5 inch
- banded black and yellow like bumble-bees (but do not sting)
- legs are dark colored

Horse Fly
Tabanidae Family
Tabanus spp.

- length: up to 0.75 inch
- compound eyes often iridescent green
- biting and usually associated with still or slow-moving water

Deer Fly
Tabanidae Family
Chrysops spp.

- length: up to 0.5 inch
- wings with dark horizontal band
- abdomen has multiple light bands

Long-legged Fly
Dolichopodidae Family
Hydrophorus spp.

- length: up to 0.25 inch
- more narrow bodied than most other fly groups with longer legs
- often metallic blue

House Fly
Muscidae Family
Musca spp.

- length: 0.25 to 0.5 inch
- common; frequently associated with human activities such as farms
- often metallic blue

Dung Fly
Scathophagidae Family
Scathophaga spp.

- length: 0.25 to 0.5 inch
- common and similar in appearance to house fly
- larvae often found in scat

Blow Fly
Calliphoridae Family
Protocalliphora spp.

- length: 0.25 to 0.5 inch
- similar to flesh flies; often metallic green or blue
- larvae found in carrion and scat

Grass Fly
Chloropidae Family
Meromyza spp.

- length: 0.125 to 0.25 inch
- colors vary but many species in this group have gray bodies with a more colorful head

Flesh Fly
Sarcophagidae Family
Sarcophaga spp.

- length: 0.5 to 0.75 inch
- thorax mottled; abdomen with three horizontal lighter stripes
- larvae scavenge off carrion

Tachinid Fly
Tachinidae Family

- length: 0.5 to 0.75 inch
- bee-like; head, thorax, and abdomen bristled with fine hairs (more so than other fly families)
- larvae parasitize other insects

Trichopoda spp.　　*Parachytas spp.*

Ephydrid Fly
Ephydridae Family

- length: 0.125 to 0.25 inch
- also known as brine flies
- found within some of Yellowstone's geothermal features

True Bug (Hemiptera) Order

This order includes cicadas, hoppers, aphids, and other true bugs. Although not as large a group as the beetles, there are over 10,000 species of Hemiptera in North America. Most species have two pairs of wings and can be distinguished from other orders by the forewings' thick base and more membranous tip.

Cicada
Cicadidae Family
Okanagana bella

- length: up to 1.5 inches
- similar to eastern cicada species but does not have mass emergences (and doesn't have red eyes)
- dark bodies with wings showing distinct venation

Cicada
Cicadidae Family
Platypedia putnami

- length: up to 1.5 inches
- similar characteristics as *Okanagana* species and, like most cicadas, the singing males are more often heard than seen

Tree Hopper
Membracidae Family

- length: 0.25 inch
- large pronotum extending over abdomen gives a humpback appearance to this group
- most are good jumpers

Thelia spp.   *Stictocephala spp.*

Leafhopper
Cicadellidae Family
Macrosteles spp.

- length: 0.25 inch
- hind leg is lined with spines
- many species are light green with stripes and/or spots along back

Aphid
Aphididae Family
Sitobion spp.

- length: 0.125 inch
- most aphids are soft bodied with a unique pair of appendages (cornicles) on the abdomen
- common garden pest
- not all species have wings

Spittlebug
Cercopidae Family
Aphrophora spp.

- length: 0.125 inch
- spittlebugs can be distinguished from leafhoppers by the presence of just one or two spines on the hind leg as opposed to a row of spines
- often covered in foamy spittle

Backswimmer
Notonectidae Family
Notonecta spp.

- length: 0.25 to 0.5 inch
- aquatic; often swims upside down
- rear legs specialized for efficient swimming
- similar to boatman species but front legs not scooped
- capable of delivering a painful bite

Water Boatman
Corixidae Family
Hesperocorixa spp.

- length: 0.25 inch
- aquatic (prefers still water)
- front legs small and scoop-like
- does not bite

Toad Bug
Gelastocoridae Family
Gelastocoris oculatus

- length: 0.25 inch
- characteristics that this bug shares with its namesake include its ability to hop, wide body, bulging eyes, and preference for muddy areas

Giant Water Bug
Belostomatidae Family
Belostoma spp.

- length: 1.25 to 1.75 inches
- flat bodied and oval shaped with pointed head and abdomen
- aquatic (prefers still water)

Water Strider
Gerridae Family
Gerris spp.

- length: 0.25 to 0.5 inch (plus long legs)
- aquatic but surface dwelling thanks to specialized hairs on lower legs
- rear upper leg segment (femur) is longer than abdomen

Assassin Bug
Reduviidae Family
Apiomerus spp.

- length: 0.25 to 0.5 inch
- color variable but often red or brown
- fine hairs cover head and thorax
- preys upon other insects, particularly bees

Assassin Bug
Reduviidae Family
Reduvius spp.

- length: 0.25 to 0.5 inch
- color red or brown
- beak is specialized for impaling prey
- long, thin antennae

Ambush Bug
Reduviidae Family
Phymata spp.

- angular bodies
- preys upon other insects and often found within flowers

Plant Bug
Miridae Family
Adelphocoris spp.

- length: 0.25 inch
- red or brown with spots behind head
- antennae usually about same length as body

Plant Bug
Miridae Family
Stenodema spp.

- length: 0.25 to 0.5 inch
- legs and antennae both long and slender
- most species herbivorous

Stink Bug
Pentatomidae Family
Thyanta spp.

- length: 0.25 to 0.5 inch
- angular (pentagon-like) body shape
- very small head with five-segmented antennae

Stink Bug
Pentatomidae Family
Brochymena spp.

- length: 0.25 to 0.5 inch
- similar to *Thyanta* species but with cryptic, bark-colored body

Leaf-footed Bug
Coreidae Family
Leptoglossus spp.

- length: up to 0.75 inch
- lower legs flattened (leaf-like)
- front wing has parallel venation

Shield-backed Bug
Scutelleridae Family
multiple genus

- length: 0.25 to 0.5 inch
- similar to stink bugs, but broader and more oval shaped
- thorax has enlarged "scutellum" covering abdomen

Boxelder Bug
Rhopalidae Family
Boisea spp.

- length: 0.5 to 0.75 inch
- often black and red colored
- unlike most true bugs, boxelders are scentless

Seed Bug
Lygaeidae Family
multiple genus

- length: 0.5 inch
- black and red, but front wing less veined than in boxelders

Butterfly & Moth (Lepidoptera) Order

This group of insects is admired by almost everyone, and a vivid butterfly undulating on the breeze somehow brightens any outdoor activity. Any of the Lepidoptera species are instantly recognizable as belonging in this order, and their bright colors and bold patterns often make them an easier group to become familiar with than other insects. Only six groups are represented in this section (gossamer-wings, swallowtails, brushfoots, whites and yellows, skippers, and moths), so learning the characteristics of each group is fairly straightforward.

Collecting insects, or even netting with the intent of release, is not allowed in national parks. Our best options, then, are to observe butterflies with binoculars or capture them with a camera.

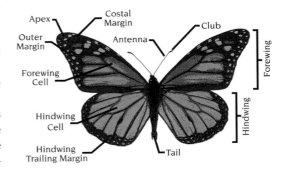

Ideal butterfly-watching binoculars allow for close focusing, and a macro lens is a great asset for insect photography. Either way, a little patience proves essential.

Many female butterflies look similar to males and have the same patterns. In some species, females appear slightly paler in color. When males and females look identical, females can sometimes be distinguished by their slightly more pronounced abdomen from carrying eggs.

We tend to pay closer attention to the adult forms of butterflies (only adults are illustrated in this section), but their life cycle progresses from egg to caterpillar to pupa and finally adulthood. Adults may live for only a few weeks. Butterflies and moths cope with this ecosystem's substantial winter in a variety of ways. Monarchs have one of the most impressive strategies, migrating over the course of several generations between Canada, the United States, and Mexico. Some species overwinter as pupa, while others, such as mourning cloaks and tortoiseshells, overwinter as adults and can be found during the coldest months underneath bark, rocks, and logs, or in the crawl spaces below buildings. Specialized proteins act as antifreeze in their circulatory system, allowing them to endure sub-freezing temperatures.

Just like any other wildlife, butterfly and moth species are usually associated with some habitats more than others. Lepidoptera are often associated more strongly with one or two plant species. In general, open areas are better butterfly habitats than forested areas, and sunny days will provide more sightings than cold, cloudy days. Other good spots to look for butterflies are on hilltops (often used as mating sites) and around mud puddles and scat (horse scat seems especially delicious to several species).

Gossamer-wing (Lycaenidae) Family

American Copper
Lycaena phlaeas

- wingspan: 1 inch
- hindwing fringed and has a wide orange stripe on trailing edge
- forewing is orange with distinct black spots underneath

Behr's Hairstreak
Satyrium behrii

- wingspan: 1 to 1.25 inches
- unlike other species of hairstreaks, this species lacks trailing hair-like tail
- when landed, subtle gray underside is visible

Greenish Blue
Plebejus saepiolus

- wingspan: 1 inch
- wings blue with white edges above and gray or white below
- females are brown above but still have dark "comma" on forewing

Lupine Blue
Plebejus lupini

- wingspan: 1 inch
- hindwing has clear orange band along trailing edge; forewing is black edged
- named for lupine color, not diet, as it prefers flowers such as buckwheat

Swallowtail (Papilionidae) Family

Western Tiger Swallowtail
Papilio rutulus

- wingspan: 3.25 inches
- large, bright, and relatively common
- male and females are similar

Pale Swallowtail
Papilio eurymedon

- wingspan: 3 to 5 inches
- similar to western tiger swallowtail but lighter and innermost bar on forewing much wider

Rocky Mountain Parnassian
Parnassius phoebus

- wingspan: 2 inches
- white wings with scattered black and red spots
- often found at high elevations flying low to the ground

Brushfoot (Nymphalidae) Family

Monarch
Danaus plexippus

- wingspan: 3.5 to 4 inches
- large, orange in color, and usually flies with wings held in an obvious V
- plant diet renders it unpalatable to predators
- very migratory (winters in Mexico)

Green Comma
Polygonia faunus

- wingspan: 1.5 to 2 inches
- wings jagged with distinct black spots
- hindwing has dark edges with small yellow spots
- underwings gray and cryptic

Pale Crescent
Phyciodes pallida

- wingspan: 1.5 inches
- large black spot in lower center of forewing is specific to pale crescents
- often found feeding on thistle flowers

Checkerspot
Euphydryas spp.

- wingspan: 1.5 inches
- wings "checkered" in patterns of orange, yellow, and black
- eye color of this genus of checkerspot is brown

Zerene Fritillary
Speyeria zerene

- wingspan: 2 to 2.5 inches
- the central spots on the forewing of this fritillary species are larger than other fritillaries
- males typically orange, but colors vary

Mormon Fritillary
Speyeria mormonia

- wingspan: 1.5 to 2 inches
- smaller than most other fritillary species with proportionally smaller forewings that may appear more rounded
- females similar to males but slightly paler

Milbert's Tortoiseshell
Nymphalis milberti

- wingspan: 1.5 to 2 inches
- this colorful butterfly has orange and yellow markings on wings with serrated edges
- gray below
- adults seen as early as March

California Tortoiseshell
Nymphalis californica

- wingspan: 1.5 to 2.5 inches
- less common in GYE than Milbert's tortoiseshell and has wings with less yellow markings and more deeply lobed edges

Mourning Cloak
Nymphalis antiopa

- wingspan: 2.25 to 3 inches
- black, blue, and yellow markings are unlike any other species
- adults first seen in spring or early summer

Red Admiral
Vanessa atalanta

- wingspan: 2.25 inches
- pattern of red stripes and white spots is unique to this species
- mostly gray below with red, white, and blue on leading edge of forewing

Painted Lady
Vanessa cardui

- wingspan: 2.25 inches
- orange overall with thick black band on central forewing and white spots
- this is the most widely distributed butterfly in the world

Weidemeyer's Admiral
Limenitis weidemeyerii

- wingspan: 2.5 to 3 inches
- black with thick white band across fore- and hindwings
- this is the only species of black and white colored butterfly in the GYE

Small Wood Nymph
Cercyonis oetus

- wingspan: 1.5 inches
- forewing has two eyespots, the lower one noticeably smaller (this differs from the common wood nymph, which is similar but spots are equal in size)

Common Alpine
Erebia epipsodea

- wingspan: 2 inches
- series of eye-spots on both fore- and hind-wings are surrounded by orange patches
- often found at higher elevations in late summer

Hayden's Ringlet
Coenonympha haydenii

- wingspan: 1.5 inches
- brown overall; underside of hindwing showing eyespots within an orange ring

underside

Arctic
Oeneis spp.

- wingspan: 1.5 to 2 inches
- several species of arctic butterflies occur in the GYE, all of which are mottled gray below; some lack eyespots
- often found at high elevations

White & Yellow (Pieridae) Family

Spring White
Pontia sisymbrii

- wingspan: 1.5 inches
- dark central bar toward the leading edge of forewing is typically more narrow than in western white
- often found on ridges and peaks

Western White
Pontia occidentalis

- wingspan: 1.75 inches
- very similar to spring white, but central bar on forewing is broader and hindwing may have light spots along trailing edge

Stella Sara Orangetip
Anthocharis sara

- wingspan: 1.5 inches
- black and yellow tips of forewing are unlike any other species
- females also have orange markings, but are paler

Olympia Marble
Euchloe olympia

- wingspan: 1.5 inches
- hindwing marbled with olive-green streaks
- antennae are white

Giant Sulphur
Colias gigantea

- wingspan: 2 inches
- black border along wing edges is wider than other sulphurs
- like most sulphurs, females have similar markings but are paler yellow

Orange Sulphur
Colias eurytheme

- wingspan: 1.75 inches
- the hindwing has two adjacent spots of different sizes underneath and centrally located
- common throughout the West

Clouded Sulphur
Colias philodice

- wingspan: 1.5 to 2 inches
- also very common but more yellow overall than orange sulphur
- forewing has clear eyespot and all wings bordered in black

Skipper (Hesperiidae) Family

Characteristics of this family include a skipping flight pattern, large bodies, angular wings, and antennae clubs that taper to a point.

Woodland Skipper
Ochlodes sylvanoides

- wingspan: 1 inch
- large oval spot on forewing
- common throughout the Rocky Mountains

Common Sootywing
Pholisora catullus

- wingspan: 1 inch
- dark with white spots toward wing tips (more abundant on forewing)
- wings often held flat when perched

Juba Skipper
Hesperia juba

- wingspan: 1.5 inches
- males mottled orange-brown above
- females similar but with hindwing bordered in black

Common Checkered Skipper
Pyrgus communis

- wingspan: 1 inch
- wings checkered black and white, with fine hairs often giving slightly blue hue to wings and body

Moths

Moths fall within the same order as butterflies but differences include their nocturnal tendencies, antennae that are feathery as opposed to clubbed, and a habit of perching with their wings folded over their bodies rather than held vertically.

Columbia Silkmoth
Hyalophora columbia

- wingspan: 3 to 4 inches
- very large with wings banded in brown, gray, and pale yellow (from body outward)
- both hind- and forewing have spots, hindwing spots are more cresent shaped

Elegant Sheepmoth
Hemileuca eglanterina

- wingspan: 2.5 to 3.5 inches
- forewings pink and hindwings orange, both with distinct bars and spots
- often seen during daytime hours

Neumoegen's Buckmoth
Hemileuca neumoegeni

- wingspan: 2 to 3 inches
- body red-orange
- wings white with zigzagging lines and crescent-shaped spots

Hera Buckmoth
Hemileuca hera

- wingspan: 3 to 3.5 inches
- paler body than Neumoegen's buckmoth and black wing markings thicker
- often associated with sagebrush habitats

Tiger Moth
Gnophaela vermiculata

- wingspan: 1.5 inches
- dark bodied and winged with very distinct white cells on all wings
- often active during the day and found on flower heads

Tiger Moth
Grammia spp.

- wingspan: 2.5 inches
- wide bodied; forewings patterned with angular markings and hindwings paler

Bruce's Tiger Moth
Neoarctia brucei

- wingspan: 2.5 inches
- similar to *Grammia* tiger moths but with less distinct markings

Bedstraw Hawkmoth
Hyles gallii

- wingspan: 2.5 to 3 inches
- beautifully marked wings with streaks of olive, gray, light yellow, and pink
- often resembles hummingbirds in flight and when feeding

Vashti Sphinx
Sphinx vashti

- wingspan: 3 to 4 inches
- very similar to bedstraw hawkmoth but larger with less distinct wing markings

Pachylioid Sphinx
Pachylioides resumens

- wingspan: 3.5 to 4 inches
- tip of forewing is pointed
- hindwing is shaded orange or pink
- seen occasionally in the southern extent of GYE

Hooded Owlet
Cucullia intermedia

- wingspan: 2 inches
- drab gray overall with long, slender wings
- thorax has hair tufts that extend over head, giving a hood-like appearance

Army Cutworm Moth
Euxoa auxiliaris

- wingspan: 2 inches
- another subtle moth with gray or brown wings (hindwing paler than forewing)
- this species of moth gathers in masses at high elevations and becomes an important food source for grizzly bears

Dart Moth
Scotogramma farnham

- wingspan: 1 inch
- drab with marbled forewing and uniformly wide body

Pandora Moth
Coloradia pandora

- wingspan: 3 inches
- dark bars on forewing zigzag vertically across wings
- hindwing typically pink with single spot
- feeds on pine needles

Red Carpet
Xanthorhoe munitata

- wingspan: 1 inch
- small bodied with long, elegant wings
- pronounced vertical bar on forewing
- often hold wings more like butterflies when at rest

Dragonfly & Damselfly (Odonata) Order

Like butterflies, dragonflies are large, colorful, and quickly recognizable as a group. These insects do not bite or sting but are phenomenally designed predators. They are some of the most agile fliers in the world, capable of flying in any direction and reaching speeds of up to 30 miles per hour. This dexterity, combined with incredibly sensitive compound eyes, makes them extremely effective predators upon smaller insects, including other dragonflies. Many species specialize in catching mosquitoes.

General characteristics of adult odonates are large heads, an extremely long and flexible abdomen consisting of 10 sections, and two pairs of wings that tend to be very similar in size to one another.

Dragonflies and damselflies are aquatic invertebrates. The majority of their lives is spent as larvae (also called nymphs) in rivers, streams, lakes, or ponds. This aquatic phase can be a few months, but in colder areas like the GYE the larval stage can take several years before metamorphosis occurs. During this time, the larvae look completely different from their adult form but are equally predatory. Odonate larvae prey upon other aquatic insects, and are also capable of catching small fish or tadpoles with a specially designed lower lip that shoots outward and captures the prey.

Once the larva grows large enough, it switches to breathing air, climbs out of the water, and emerges from its larval case. Soon after, the adult is capable of flight and is ready to hunt, find a mate, and continue its life cycle.

Damselfly (Zygoptera) Suborder

Damselflies have a similar lifestyle to dragonflies but have a very narrow abdomen, and, when at rest, adults fold their wings together over their body rather than spreading them out to the sides.

Almost all of the species in this group are metallic green or blue, with females being duller overall and having a pronounced ovipositor. Coloration does not vary seasonally, but eye color changes throughout an individual's life.

Damselfly nymphs are slender and have three feathery gills at the tip of the abdomen. A secondary advantage to having oxygen transfer posteriorly is that they are capable of expelling water quickly, launching them from place to place. Nymphs also transport themselves by waving their gills or by undulating their entire bodies.

damselfly nymph

River Jewelwing
Calopterygidae Family
Calopteryx aequabilis

- length: 2 to 2.5 inches
- males metallic green with wide black wingtips
- females are less metallic with light brown wings that are more evenly colored

Spotted Spreadwing
Lestidae Family
Lestes congener

- length: 1.5 inches
- both males and females dull brown; male's eyes blue, female's eyes brown
- ventral side of thorax has a pair of dark spots

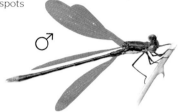

Emerald Spreadwing
Lestidae Family
Lestes dryas

- length: 1.5 inches
- males and females both metallic green with females less colored ventrally; both have relatively stocky thoraxes

Tule Bluet
Coenagrionidae Family
Enallagma carunculatum

- length: 1 to 1.5 inches
- male entirely blue except for darker section midway along abdomen; eyes blue
- females usually have all dark abdomen with light-brown eyes

Northern Bluet
Coenagrionidae Family
Enallagma annexum

- length: 1 to 1.5 inches
- males entirely blue with black bars and blue and black eyes
- females typically brown but some are blue; eyes are brown

Western Forktail
Coenagrionidae Family
Ischnura perparva

- length: 1.25 inches
- males have mostly black abdomen with blue tip; eyes green and black
- female bodies may be orange when young, eventually becoming uniformly gray

Vivid Dancer
Coenagrionidae Family
Argia vivida

- length: 1 to 1.75 inches
- males similar to Paiute dancer but with less black on head and much more blue along abdomen
- females may appear similar to males or all brown

Paiute Dancer
Coenagrionidae Family
Argia alberta

- length: 1 to 1.5 inches
- males have black markings on head that extend into eye stripes within blue eyes; thorax with wide black stripe and abdomen mostly dark
- females typically all brown or pale blue

Dragonfly (Anisoptera) Suborder

Dragonfly species are generally similar in appearance and lifestyle to damselflies and are most frequently encountered near still water. Overall, dragonflies appear more robust than damselflies in both adult and nymph forms, with a wider head, thorax, and abdomen. Dragonflies tend to hold wings out to the side when at rest, and the tip of the adult's abdomen has three appendages where damselflies have four.

Dragonfly nymphs are also similar to damselfly nymphs, but their larger size allows them to stalk bigger prey. They also breathe through gills located at the end of the abdomen that facilitate both oxygen exchange and propulsion, but their gills aren't feathery like those of damselflies.

The images below show two common types of dragonfly nymphs. Darner dragonfly nymphs are relatively cylindrical and have abdomens that taper to a distinct point. Skimmer dragonfly nymphs are broader overall and have scoop-shaped mouthparts.

darner dragonfly nymph   skimmer dragonfly nymph

Lance-tipped Darner
Aeshnidae Family
Aeshna constricta

- length: 2.75 inches
- characteristics of the genus *Aeshna* are two stripes down front of thorax as well as two diagonal stripes down the side
- male coloration can be blue or green; females similar or pale yellow

♂

Paddle-tailed Darner
Aeshnidae Family
Aeshna palmata

- length: 2.75 inches
- very similar to lance-tipped darner but may have more green markings and has a slender line horizontally across face
- females have similar markings but are often paler

♂

Shadow Darner
Aeshnidae Family
Aeshna umbrosa

- length: 2.75 inches
- marks similar to other darners but with more slender stripes and spots, giving a darker appearance overall
- spots along abdomen relatively small and face lacks line found in paddle-tailed darners

♂

Common Green Darner
Aeshnidae Family
Anax junius

- length: 3 inches
- this is the only darner species in the GYE with green head, green thorax, and blue abdomen
- females have similar markings but often with brown abdomen; both sexes have maroon abdomens shortly after emergence

♂

American Emerald
Corduliidae Family
Cordulia shurtleffii

- length: 1.75 inches
- both sexes similar with brown thorax and abdomen (which widens toward tip) and bright green eyes

♀

♂

Common Whitetail
Libellulidae Family
Plathemis lydia

- length: 2.75 inches
- male patterns are unlike any other dragonfly with dark head, all-white tail, and thick wing bands
- females differ in having a brown abdomen and three dark spots on each wing

♂

Flame Skimmer
Libellulidae Family
Libellula saturata

- length: 2.25 inches
- nearly every part of the male is brilliant orange except the outer wings
- females much more brown with some orange venation in wings

♂

Twelve-spotted Skimmer
Libellulidae Family
Libellula pulchella

- length: 2.25 inches
- males wings have three large dark spots and four white spots on each wing; abdomen pale blue to white
- females have similar wing patterns but lacking white spots; brown abdomens
- eight-spotted skimmers also found here; very similar except for number of spots

♂

Dot-tailed Whiteface
Libellulidae Family
Leucorrhinia intacta

- length: 1.25 inches
- head, thorax, and abdomen all dark with diagnostic isolated yellow dot toward tip of abdomen
- females often more brown but still have yellow dot

♂

White-faced Meadowhawk
Libellulidae Family
Sympetrum obtrusum

- length: 1.5 inches
- males have white faces, red eyes, red thorax, and red abdomen with black triangular markings laterally
- females are brown but abdominal markings usually visible

♂

Cherry-faced Meadowhawk
Libellulidae Family
Sympetrum internum

- length: 1.25 inches
- very similar in size and markings to white-faced meadowhawk but with red face instead of white
- base of wings may be slightly reddish
- females brown or olive colored

♂

Band-winged Meadowhawk
Libellulidae Family
Sympetrum semicinctum

- length: 1.25 inches
- males resemble other meadowhawks but with much more red along the base of wings and with less black markings along abdomen
- females brown or yellow with more dark markings on abdomen than males

♂

Mayfly (Ephemeroptera) Order

This order of aquatic insects is important both ecologically and economically to our region. Trout rely on mayflies as one of their primary food sources within the Rocky Mountains; consequently this is one of the most common insects that fly-fishing anglers replicate when pursuing their prey.

Mayfly larvae typically have three tails, but a few species have two, and all species have one claw extending from each leg. These larvae tend to feed upon detritus within rivers and streams, and have leaf-like gills for oxygen intake along the abdomen.

Adult mayflies are recognized by their tendency to hold their wings upright as opposed to flat across their bodies. These adults have two phases made up of duns (also known as subimagos), which last an hour to up to three days, and spinners (adults). The adult phase can reproduce but is unable to feed. This family's name comes from "ephemeral," due to its short-lived adult phase, which lasts one to two days.

Blue-winged Olive
Baetidae Family
Baetis tricaudatus

- length: up to 0.5 inch
- a common species replicated by fly-fishing anglers due to its abundance
- nymphs tend to have oval-shaped gills and antennae two to three times the length of the head

larva

Pale Morning Dun
Ephemeridae Family
Drunella spp.

- length: up to 0.75 inch
- this genus of mayflies is one of the most common in the GYE
- abundant in dammed waters including beaver ponds and reservoirs

larva

Western Drake
Ephemeridae Family
Ephemerella spp.

- length: up to 0.75 inch
- western drakes are common in the GYE
- often found in slow-moving waters including dammed habitats

larva

Flathead Mayfly
Heptageniidae Family
Rhithrogena spp.

- length: up to 0.5 inch
- legs and body more flattened than other aquatic invertebrates
- eyes and mouthparts located dorsally

larva

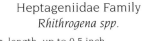

Stonefly (Plecoptera) Order

Stoneflies are an aquatic group of insects that are distinct in both their larval and adult stages. As larvae, they are commonly found in fast-moving, cold water with high oxygen content. Stonefly larvae are stocky and have two long antennae, two long tails, and legs with two claws. During this aquatic stage, oxygen is taken in through gills located at the base of the thorax. Some species feed on detritus and others feed on smaller invertebrates. A stonefly's life cycle typically takes less than one year, but a few take two to three years.

Adult stoneflies generally resemble the larvae, and both stages have two tails and long antennae. Their four wings are membranous and fold flat across the thorax, usually extending beyond the abdomen.

Stoneflies are ecologically important for several reasons: they break down plant matter in rivers, serve as prey to a wide variety of other animals, and function as indicators of water quality due to their sensitivity to pollution. Both the adults and larvae are replicated by fly-fishing anglers and can also be used as live bait where allowed. Lengths given below exclude wings, antennae, and tail.

Green Stonefly
Chloroperlidae Family
Sweltsa spp.

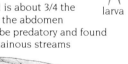

- length: 0.25 to 0.5 inch
- body more cylindrical than other stoneflies
- larval tail is about 3/4 the length of the abdomen   larva
- tends to be predatory and found in mountainous streams

Golden Stonefly
Perlidae Family
Hesperoperla spp.

- length: up to 0.5 inch
- flattened, dark body with yellow markings
- requires moving water to oxygenate gills   larva
- opportunistic predator upon a wide variety of other aquatic invertebrates

Perlodid (Giant) Stonefly
Perlodidae Family
Isoperla spp.

- length: up to 0.25 inch
- body flattened; head and thorax usually dark brown with yellow lines
- life cycle typically takes place within one year with adults emerging in early summer   larva

Salmon Fly
Pteronarcyidae Family
Pteronarcella badia

- length: up to 0.5 inch
- body slightly cylindrical and dark brown in coloration
- in larval stages, the thoracic plates project outward more than other stoneflies   larva
- adults emerge in early summer

Caddisfly (Trichoptera) Order

Many of the members of this order of insects are incredible architects in their aquatic stages, building intricate housings out of unlikely materials such as pebbles, sand, and conifer needles. This construction is possible due to their ability to create silky thread, binding these materials together. Most caddisflies have a one-year life cycle, with adults living one to four weeks.

The common categories of caddisflies include saddle-case caddisflies (larvae build dome-shaped cases that cover them completely except for openings at each end), net-spinners, tube-case caddisflies (build portable cases they drag with them), free-living caddisflies (don't build cases), and purse-case caddisflies (build cases of fine silk and sand).

A primary distinction between adult caddisflies and other aquatic invertebrates is that the adult caddisflies fold their wings over their backs in a tent-shaped profile. Other anatomical differences include elongated bodies, very short antennae, and only one claw on each leg.

Humpless Casemaker Caddisfly
Brachycentridae Family
Amiocentrus spp.

- length: less than 0.25 inch
- often found in more slow-moving water with cases made from vegetation in horizontal patterns

larva

Little Black Caddisfly
Glossosomatidae Family
Glossosoma spp.

- length: less than 0.25 inch
- nymphs tend to make dome-shaped cases out of small pebbles

larva

Netspinning Caddisfly
Hydropsychidae Family
Hydropsyche spp.

- length: less than 0.25 inch
- often without a case, builds threaded nets in moving waters to trap prey

larva

Bizzare Caddisfly
Lepidostomatidae Family
Lepidostoma spp.

- length: less than 0.25 inch
- larval cases typically made out of pebbles or, occasionally, vegetation
- larvae have distinct hump on front abdominal segment

larva

Net-tube Caddisfly
Psychomyiidae Family
Psychomyia spp.

- length: less than 0.5 inch
- larvae have obvious large front legs
- cases built permanently underground or in vegetative debris

Free-living Caddisfly
Rhyacophilidae Family
Rhyacophila spp.

- length: less than 0.5 inch
- larvae caseless and found in fast-moving water

larva

Sawfly, Bee, Wasp, & Ant (Hymenoptera) Order

This group of insects varies widely in appearance, but most species are equipped with two pairs of wings, with the forewing larger than the hindwing. Many species of Hymenoptera have sophisticated social communities.

Cimbicid Sawfly
Cimbicidae Family
Cimbex spp.

- length: up to 0.75 inch
- similar to bumble bees but with clubbed antennae

Common Sawfly
Tenthredinidae Family
Tenthredo spp.

- length: 0.25 to 0.5 inch
- resemble wasps but lack the narrow waist common in wasp species

Horntail
Siricidae Family
Tremex spp.

- length: 0.75 to 1.5 inches
- abdominal projection (horn) is characteristic and is non-stinging

Cuckoo Wasp
Chrysididae Family
Chrysis spp.

- length: 0.125 to 0.25 inch
- typically metallic green or blue
- name comes from habit of laying eggs in other insects' nests (as cuckoo birds do in other birds' nests)

Chalcidoid Wasp
Chalcididae Family
Leucospis spp.

- length: 0.125 to 0.25 inch
- yellow and black coloration on thorax and abdomen
- long ovipositor that extends forward from tip of abdomen to thorax

Braconid Wasp
Braconidae Family
Apanteles spp.

- length: 0.125 to 0.25 inch
- longer antennae than most other wasps
- female has very long, narrow ovipositor

Ichneumonid Wasp
Ichneumonidae Family
Bathyplectes anurus

- length: 0.125 to 0.25 inch
- similar in characteristics to many other wasps but usually has longer antennae and ovipositor

Ichneumonid Wasp
Ichneumonidae Family
Megarhyssa icterosticta

- length: 0.75 inch plus very long tail
- large size, long tail and ovipositor, and narrow waist are all characteristic

Thread-waisted Wasp
Sphecidae Family
Ammophila spp.

- length: up to 0.75 inch
- very narrow waisted and typically with orange on the abdomen

Thread-waisted Wasp
Sphecidae Family
Prionyx spp.

- length: up to 0.5 inch
- all dark, narrow waisted, and wider abdomen than other wasps

Square-headed Wasp
Crabronidae Family
Tachytes spp.

- length: 0.25 to 0.5 inch
- large, angular head
- preys upon flies and often seen on flowers

Apoid Wasp
Crabronidae Family
Cerceris spp.

- length: 0.5 to 0.75 inch
- large, angular head with abdomen black and yellow striped
- many species prey upon beetles

Bumble Bee
Apidae Family
Bombus spp.

- length: up to 1 inch
- head, thorax, and abdomen all robust and hairy

Metallic Green Bee
Halictidae Family
Agapostemon spp.

- length: up to 0.5 inch
- relatively small bee with subtle metallic green thorax
- often nests underground

Leaf-cutting Bee
Megachilidae Family
Megachile spp.

- length: 0.25 to 0.5 inch
- broad head and thorax
- cuts uniform round segments from leaves

Honey Bee
Apidae Family
Apis mellifera

- length: 0.25 to 0.5 inch
- dense hairs across thorax, head, and eyes
- introduced from Europe
- commonly cultivated for honey and as pollinating agents

Blue-black Spider Wasp
Pompilidae Family
Anoplius spp.

- length: 0.5 to 0.75 inch
- all dark except for occasional orange markings on abdomen
- long legged
- preys on spiders; inflicts painful sting

Spider Wasp
Pompilidae Family
Auplopus spp.

- length: 0.5 to 0.75 inch
- similar in description to *Anoplius* wasps to left but often more metallic blue in color and is more likely to create nests out of mud

Spider Wasp
Pompilidae Family
Ageniella spp.

- length: 0.5 to 0.75 inch
- more orange bodied than other spider wasps (some species have orange abdomen only)

Spider Wasp
Pompilidae Family
Aporus spp.

- length: 0.5 to 0.75 inch
- both sexes dark overall, but females slightly larger

Velvet Ant
Mutillidae Family
Dasymutilla spp.

- length: 0.5 to 0.75 inch
- red and black and covered with many fine hairs
- males have wings, females wingless
- can inflict painful sting

♂   ♀

Prairie Yellowjacket
Vespidae Family
Vespula atropilosa

- length: up to 1 inch
- abdomen banded yellow and black with small yellow marking on face
- common; one of the most likely wasps to sting people

Paper Wasp
Vespidae Family
Polistes spp.

- length: 0.5 to 0.75 inch
- more brown, less yellow, and longer legs than yellow-jackets
- named for papery nests

Tiphiid Wasp
Tiphiidae Family
Myzinum spp.

- length: 1 to 1.25 inches
- males more slender than females and with less curved antennae
- both thorax and abdomen banded black and yellow

Carpenter Ant
Formicidae Family
Camponotus spp.

- length: 0.25 to 0.5 inch
- larger than most other ant groups with some individuals winged and others (typically worker ants) wingless
- capable of biting and stinging

Formica Ant
Formicidae Family
Formica spp.

- length: 0.25 to 0.5 inch
- many species are all red and others have darker abdomens
- common in forested areas or other habitats where materials are readily available for building mounds

Harvester Ant
Formicidae Family
Pogonomyrmex spp.

- length: 0.25 to 0.5 inch
- all members of this group have a beard-like structure beneath head
- one of the most toxic venoms of any insect

Springtail (Collembola) Order

Also known as snow fleas, springtails are tiny insects that are most noticeable when they emerge onto the surface of the snow in winter. They are harmless and make their living in forested areas as decomposers of organic material.

Springtail
Hypogastrura spp.

- length: 0.125
- this species of springtail is dark and elongated; others are almost spherical in body shape
- many species of springtails have the ability to jump long distances due to a specialized appendage (furcula) that projects them forward

Spider (Araneae) Order

Spiders differ from insects in that they have two main body parts rather than three, eight legs rather than six, and no antennae. Many species of spiders are web-makers and let their prey come to them, while others actively pursue their prey. Most spiders inject venom to immobilize prey, but they prefer to avoid people. The infamously poisonous brown recluse is not known to inhabit this region.

Bold Jumper
Salticidae Family
Phidippus audax

- length: 0.25 to 0.5 inch
- black with three white spots on abdomen

Trashline Orbweaver
Araneidae Family
Cyclosa conica

- length: 0.25 inch
- abdomen uniquely tapered toward end
- this group of spiders makes the classic web of concentric circles

Long-jawed Orbweaver
Tetragnathidae Family
Tetragnatha versicolor

- length: 0.125 to 0.5 inch
- very long legs and narrow bodies
- webs often built above water

Goldenrod Crab Spider
Thomisidae Family
Misumena vatia

- length: 0.125 to 0.25 inch
- female pale yellow with red stripes along sides
- males are more brown colored with two pairs of yellow hind legs

♀

Grass Spider
Agelenidae Family
Agelenopsis spp.

- length: up to 0.5 inch
- mostly brown with stripes vertical to body length
- webs are funnel shaped

Hobo Spider
Agelenidae Family
Tegenaria agrestis

- length: up to 0.5 inch
- coloration and markings subtle making accurate identification difficult
- abdomen has slight pale V markings
- native to Europe but has gained a nasty reputation here for its potent venom despite typical shy tendencies

Wolf Spider
Lycosidae Family
Pardosa spp.

- length: up to 1.5 inches
- mottled gray with eight irregularly shaped eyes and delicate claws at the tips of each leg
- typically hunt at night and do not create webs

Other Invertebrates

Rocky Mountain Wood Tick
Ixodidae Family
Dermacentor andersoni

- length: up to 0.125 inch
- brown, flattened body
- parasitic on mammals, typically feeding for three days before becoming fully engorged and dropping off
- may transmit spotted fever and other diseases

Stone Centipede
Lithobiomorpha Order
Lithobius forficatus

- length: up to 2 inches
- bodies are reddish brown and flattened
- typically have 18 body segments and 15 pairs of legs

Northern Scorpion
Paruroctonus boreus

- length: 1 to 1.5 inches
- not commonly seen in the GYE but present here and widespread throughout the West (as far north as southern Canada)
- typically light brown in color with large pinchers and characteristic scorpion body and tail

Rocky Mountain Snail
Oreohelix strigosa

- shell diameter: up to 1 inch
- usually light brown with darker brown spiraling bands
- bleached shells are often found on the ground and are more commonly seen than live snails

Amphibians

Amphibians in this region include salamanders, toads, and frogs. The plates below represent local amphibians as terrestrial adults, but the larval stage of their lives is spent aquatically. As a result, ponds, lakes, and moist areas are the best places to look for them.

Blotched Tiger Salamander
Ambystoma tigrinum melanostictum

- up to 9 inches long
- smooth skin with mottled coloration, often olive, brown, and black

Boreal Chorus Frog
Pseudacris maculata

- 1.5 inches long
- three stripes along back
- very vocal during early summer
- small pads at the tip of each toe

American Bullfrog
Lithobates catesbeianus

- up to 6 inches long
- non-native to GYE; introduced into Kelly Warm Springs, GTNP

Columbia Spotted Frog
Rana luteiventris

- up to 4 inches long
- only frog with salmon-colored legs underneath
- webbed rear feet

Boreal Toad
Anaxyrus boreas

- up to 5 inches long
- skin with distinct warty texture
- eyes with horizontal pupils

Reptiles

Due to their cold-blooded (ectothermic) nature and this region's climate, very few species of reptiles are present in the GYE. Unlike amphibians, reptiles have dry, scaly skin and don't have an aquatic stage to their development. Other reptiles common elsewhere, such as turtles, are not present here. The only poisonous snake found in this ecosystem is the prairie rattlesnake, which is restricted to a small area in north-west Yellowstone and has never been recorded in Jackson Hole.

Northern Sagebrush Lizard
Sceloporus graciosus

- up to 5 inches long
- uncommon but may be found at lower-elevation geothermal areas such as Norris and Mammoth
- dry skin with scales
- toes with claws

Rubber Boa
Charina bottae

- up to 2.5 feet long
- a harmless and beautiful snake that, upon initial appearance, resembles a large earthworm
- smooth "rubbery" skin ranges in color from brown to olive
- tail resembles head, which may be used to feign an attack against predators or aggressive prey

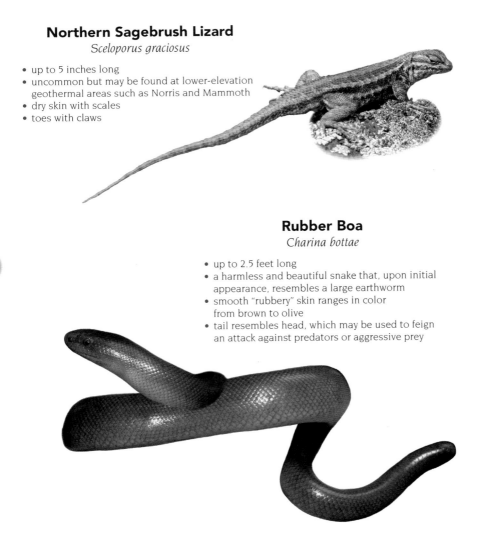

Gopher (Bull) Snake
Pituophis catenifer

- up to 6 feet long (region's largest snake)
- found in northern Yellowstone and lower elevations on the outskirts of the GYE
- smaller head than rattlesnakes and no rattle

Wandering Garter Snake
Thamnophis elegans vagrans

- up to 2 feet long
- most commonly seen reptile in GYE
- markings include dark checkered pattern and three yellow stripes running length of body (one on top and one along each side)
- typically found near water; good swimmers

Prairie Rattlesnake
Crotalus viridis

- up to 4 feet long
- in GYE, most sightings are in northwest Yellowstone in the Mammoth area, but may occur elsewhere
- bodies are typically light brown with darker brown markings along back
- larger, more triangular head than bull snakes with a narrower, rattle-tipped tail
- venomous

Fish

As a group, fish comprise the greatest number of vertebrate species in the world, with over 30,000 species known globally and over 2,000 in the United States. More than 40

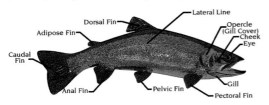

percent of these are freshwater species, a disproportionate ratio over saltwater species considering that less than one percent of the planet's water is fresh and only a fraction of this is available in unfrozen liquid habitat such as lakes, ponds, rivers, and streams. Due to the GYE's overall high elevations, recent glaciation, and cold temperatures, the ecosystem here is home to relatively few fish. Only 18 species of fish are known to inhabit these waters, and six of these are introduced, primarily as game fish.

Fish are an important food resource to many other species of wildlife including pelicans, osprey, eagles, otters, bears, and other fish. Additionally, sportfishing is a common recreational activity and brings in millions of dollars annually to the region. To support sportfishing, several species have been intentionally introduced into local lakes and rivers. These include many of the trout species such as rainbow, brook, brown, and lake trout.

Lake trout in Yellowstone Lake demonstrate how non-native species can devastate an ecosystem. These fish are native to the Great Lakes region of North America and were first discovered in Yellowstone Lake in 1994, having been introduced illegally by an unknown source. Lake trout are larger and more aggressive than native cutthroat trout and have reduced the native fish substantially. This has had a cascading effect on other species because lake trout don't spawn in Yellowstone Lake's tributaries and consequently don't provide food for other predators such as grizzly bears. Intensive efforts are underway to remove lake trout from Yellowstone Lake, although complete eradication may be impossible.

An interesting and isolated population of fish live in Grand Teton National Park's Kelly Warm Springs. This small pool maintains temperatures in the 70s Fahrenheit year-round and, consequently, several species of tropical fish released from home aquariums have survived and seem to thrive here (see page 41). These non-native species pose no threat of invading other local waters because they would not long survive outside the springs' "tropical" environment.

Sculpin (Cottidae) Family

Mottled Sculpin
Cottus bairdi

- 4 to 6 inches long
- large flat head with eyes located more dorsally than most other fish
- dorsal fin is very spiny
- tend to be bottom dwellers

Sucker (Catostomidae) Family

Longnose Sucker
Catostomus catostomus griseus

- up to 18 inches long
- long, pointed snout
- all suckers are toothless with a more ventrally placed mouth than other fish

Mountain Sucker
Catostomus platyrhynchus

- 7 to 8 inches long
- very smooth scales with proportionally longer anal fin

Utah Sucker
Catostomus ardens

- up to 24 inches long
- ventral view of mouth shows lower lip with deep median groove

Minnow (Cyprinidae) Family

Lake Chub
Couesius plumbeus

- up to 6 inches long
- body with overall dusky coloration

Utah Chub
Gila atraria

- up to 20 inches long
- bluish to brass colored above and silvery below

Speckled Dace
Rhinichthys osculus

- up to 4 inches long
- somewhat triangular head with slight hump
- gray or brown overall with dark flecks along sides

Longnose Dace
Rhinichthys cataractae

- up to 5 inches long
- elongated snout with body coloration darker above and silvery below

Redside Shiner
Richardsonius balteatus

- up to 6 inches long
- dark above, silver sides can be red-orange in breeding males

Trout (Salmonidae) Family

Species within the Salmonidae family (including trout) are important both ecologically and economically. Underwater, trout are top predators, while serving as prey to less aquatic animals such as bears, osprey, eagles, and river otters. Many popular game fish, including brown trout, rainbow trout, brook trout, and lake trout, are not native to this region.

Yellowstone Cutthroat Trout
Oncorhynchus clarkii bouvieri

- spots larger and fewer than westslope cutthroat
- pure strains found throughout Yellowstone and in upper sections of the Snake River

Snake River Finespotted Cutthroat Trout
Oncorhynchus clarkii behnkei

- heavily "peppered" with very small spots
- native range was from Jackson Lake to Palisades Reservoir, within the range of Yellowstone cutthroats
- tends to be found in faster-moving water than other cutthroat subspecies

Westslope Cutthroat Trout
Oncorhynchus clarkii lewisi

- fewer spots toward front, with spots arcing from anal fin to pectoral fin
- found in the northwest portion of the GYE (western Montana to northern Idaho)
- generally less predatory upon other fish than most cutthroat subspecies

Rainbow Trout
Oncorhynchus mykiss

- sides speckled and streaked pink
- native to waters west of the Rocky Mountains but stocked extensively in cold waters throughout North America
- anadromous (migrating between marine and fresh water) in coastal areas

Eastern Brook Trout
Salvelinus fontinalis

- back has mottled streaks on dark background
- sides are often speckled with dark or red spots
- native to waters east of the Mississippi River but stocked extensively in the West

Brown Trout
Salmo trutta

- caudal (tail) fin has no spots or very few on top
- spots along back and sides are dark and large
- native to Europe but stocked in many western lakes and rivers

Lake Trout
Salvelinus namaycush

- dark body with white spots
- up to 36 inches long and 80 pounds
- native to the Great Lakes region and some waters in Montana
- intense efforts to remove introduced lake trout from Yellowstone Lake may never completely eradicate this population

Montana Grayling
Thymallus arcticus montanus

- dorsal fin as long or longer than head
- iridescent silver body with darker spots along sides
- native to arctic regions of North America and a small area in Montana
- found in Cascade, Grebe, and Wolf Lakes in Yellowstone

Mountain Whitefish
Prosopium williamsoni

- up to 15 inches long
- gray or bronze back and silver sides, fins often black-tipped
- native to many areas within the GYE including the Snake and Yellowstone Rivers

Birds

This unique group of vertebrates is made up of over 10,000 species across the globe and over 800 within North America. Of these, about 320 or so have been documented within the Greater Yellowstone Ecosystem. This section provides plates and identification suggestions for the most commonly encountered birds within the region.

Birds have several characteristics that define them as a group, the most notable simply being the fact that the vast majority of them (all species on this continent) can fly. This ability is due primarily to the anatomical phenomena known as feathers, but many other aspects of their anatomy and physiology contribute to this critical means of travel. Feathers are a profoundly complicated form of keratin, the same material that forms a bird's bill and claws. In addition to making flight possible, feathers also are critical in providing insulation, and their coloration (or ability to refract light) aids in camouflage and attracting a mate. All feathers wear over time and are replaced through molting. Many songbirds molt twice per year and consequently their appearance changes from breeding to non-breeding seasons. Other adaptations allowing for bird flight include very lightweight bones, an ability to lay eggs (which allows chicks to develop most of their body weight outside of the female), and an exceptionally efficient respiratory system.

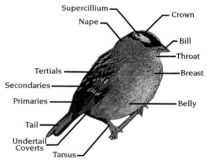

When attempting to identify an unknown bird, observe as many of its characteristics as possible and note where it was seen. When somebody asks me to help identify a bird they recently saw, my first question is inevitably, "what kind of habitat did you see it in?" Most bird species have a strong affiliation with one particular type of habitat. Knowing this immediately eliminates other species less likely to have been found there. There are many field marks to pay attention to, but two of the most important are the approximate size of the bird and the general impression of the bird's bill. Most people are familiar with the American robin, so this is a good starting point for comparison: was the mystery bird bigger or smaller than a robin? The bill of every bird is designed to be both an intake for food as well as a specialized tool. This means that bills vary widely in appearance based on their function and can be a key part of identification. The images below contrast some of the extreme bill designs found in this region and illustrate their vastly different shapes depending on whether they are for probing (curlew), tearing flesh (eagle), cracking seeds (grosbeak), or extracting nectar from flowers (hummingbird).

In addition to bird identification by physical characteristics, it is also possible to identify most species by their distinct vocalizations, which can be classified into calls and songs. Calls tend to be heard year-round, are less complicated than songs, and are associated with a particular behavior such as flight, alarm, or contact with another bird. Songs are usually more elaborate and associated with breeding or establishment of territory. Songs are more commonly heard in the spring and summer. Learning to identify birds by sound requires a lot of patience and can be overwhelming, but becoming familiar with a handful of bird songs and calls is a great foundation. Some of the highly vocal birds from this region worth learning are trumpeter swan, sandhill crane, red-tailed hawk, bald eagle, great-horned owl, belted kingfisher, northern flicker, black-billed magpie, common raven, black-capped chickadee, American robin, yellow warbler, western meadowlark, and yellow-headed blackbird.

The majority of birds represented in this guide are found within the Greater Yellowstone Ecosystem only during spring, summer, and early fall. Long winters motivate most species to migrate to warmer climates. Some fly moderate distances, wintering in the southwestern states, but others, such as the osprey, cross multiple international borders to over-winter as far away as South America. The birds found in the GYE during winter months are all hardy species, very well insulated, and worthy of our respect for surviving in such harsh conditions. If a bird is regularly seen during winter, this is mentioned in the species descriptions that follow. Otherwise it can be assumed that the species is less likely to be seen during the GYE's coldest months.

Despite a relatively low number of different species in and around Yellowstone and Grand Teton, finding birds can still be a highlight of any excursion into these national parks. Check with any of the visitor centers in the area to get current suggestions of the best places to view birds.

In the following section WS represents "wingspan," and ♂ indicates "male" and ♀ indicates "female" when species are sexually dimorphic (males and females appear differently).

Pelican (Pelecanidae) Family

American White Pelican
Pelecanus erythrorhynchos

- WS: up to 105 inches (largest wingspan in GYE)
- all white with black wing feathers visible in flight
- unlike brown pelicans, white pelicans do not plunge dive for fish, instead foraging with their large bill from the water's surface

Common Loon
Gaviidae Family
Gavia immer

- WS: 46 inches
- dark head with distinct red eye
- sharp, thick bill for catching fish
- very loud, distinct wailing call

Double-crested Cormorant
Phalacrocoracidae Family
Phalacrocorax auritus

- WS: 52 inches
- breeding adults have white "crests" on top of head
- excellent divers and fishers

Grebe (Podicipedidae) Family

Pied-billed Grebe
Podilymbus podiceps

- WS: 16 inches
- dark eye and distinct thick bill
- breeding adults have a white bill with dark band

Eared Grebe
Podiceps nigricollis

- WS: 16 inches
- unmistakable yellow plumes during breeding
- much sharper bill than pied-billed grebe

Western Grebe
Aechmophorus occidentalis

- WS: 24 inches
- bright red eye surrounded by dark "cap"
- bill color is dull yellow or olive

Clark's Grebe
Aechmophorus clarkii

- WS: 24 inches
- dark "cap" is above bright red eye
- bill is brighter yellow than western grebe

Waterfowl (Anatidae) Family

This group of birds is usually found in or near water and most feed on shallow aquatic plants or invertebrates. Some, like mergansers, dive for fish. Males tend to have more distinct or colorful plumage.

Tundra Swan
Cygnus columbianus

- WS: 66 inches
- smaller and less common than trumpeter swans
- often with yellow at base of bill (lores)

Trumpeter Swan
Cygnus buccinator

- WS: 80 inches
- Cygnets (immatures) are brown
- weigh up to 24 pounds
- longer neck and bill than tundra swan
- present year-round

cygnet

adult

Canada Goose
Branta canadensis

- WS: 55 to 60 inches
- black neck, white cheek marks, and brown body
- present year-round

Snow Goose
Chen caerulescens

- WS: 53 inches
- white with black wing tips
- arctic nester; migrates through GYE

Mallard
Anas platyrhynchos

- WS: 35 inches
- common year-round
- GYE's largest duck
- feeds by "dabbling" (tips upside-down rather than diving)

♀

♂

Gadwall
Anas strepera

- WS: 33 inches
- male plumage is subtle but patterns are distinct upon close observation
- females resemble female mallards
- present year-round

♀

♂

Green-winged Teal
Anas crecca

- WS: 23 inches
- small duck but very fast in flight

Cinnamon Teal
Anas cyanoptera

- WS: 22 inches
- breeding male dark red overall

Blue-winged Teal
Anas discors

- WS: 23 inches
- females almost identical to female cinnamon teals

Lesser Scaup
Aythya affinis

- WS: 25 inches
- similar to ring-necked duck but with all-gray bill

Ring-necked Duck
Aythya collaris

- WS: 25 inches
- black-tipped bill with white ring in breeding males
- head often with slight "crest"

Common Goldeneye
Bucephala clangula

- WS: 26 inches
- circular white patch on cheek of breeding males
- females have less yellow on bill than female Barrow's goldeneye

Bufflehead
Bucephala albeola

- WS: 21 inches
- breeding males have distinct white wedge on back of head
- present year-round

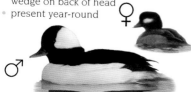

Barrow's Goldeneye
Bucephala islandica

- WS: 28 inches
- crescent-shaped white patch on cheek of breeding males
- present year-round
- more prevalent than common goldeneye

American Wigeon
Anas americana

- WS: 32 inches
- white mohawk and iridescent green behind eye distinct on breeding males

Common Merganser
Mergus merganser

- WS: 34 inches
- long body and serrated bill for diving after fish
- found on fast- and slow-moving water

Harlequin Duck
Histrionicus histrionicus

- WS: 26 inches
- elaborate markings on males
- uncommon but occasionally seen in turbulent water of Yellowstone River

Hooded Merganser
Lophodytes cucullatus

- WS: 24 inches
- very distinct head shape
- seen more frequently in winter

Northern Shoveler
Anas clypeata

- WS: 30 inches
- enormous bills on males and females used for filtering mud and water

Northern Pintail
Anas acuta

- WS: 34 inches
- long bodied, long necked; distinct pointed tail feathers
- seen only occasionally in GYE including winter

Ruddy Duck
Oxyura jamaicensis

- WS: 18 inches
- cinnamon body, facial markings, and blue bill make breeding males unmistakable
- both males and females have "stiff" tails frequently held upright

Redhead
Aythya americana

- WS: 29 inches
- males and females both have light blue or gray bill with black tip
- easily confused with canvasback duck (not shown), which is much less common in GYE

Heron, Ibis, Crane, & Coot Families

Great Blue Heron
Ardea herodias

- WS: 72 inches
- usually solitary; seen hunting along rivers and ponds
- loud croaking call often heard in flight
- flies with neck tucked unlike sandhill cranes, which fly with elongated neck
- present year-round but less common in winter

White-faced Ibis
Plegadis falcinellus

- WS: 36 inches
- red eye and face surrounded by white outline
- occasional visitor to marshy areas of GYE
- breeding males and females identical

Sandhill Crane
Grus canadensis

- WS: 75 inches
- very tall with red crown
- found in open meadows throughout GYE during spring, summer, and fall
- males and females identical and may appear rust-colored due to deliberate "staining" of feathers
- flies with neck extended
- vocalization is a loud and frequent warble, projecting great distances
- the whooping crane (not shown) is taller and all white (one of the rarest birds in North America, any whooping crane sightings should be reported)

"stained" form

American Coot
Fulica americana

- WS: 24 inches
- white, sturdy bill and distinct red eye
- toes are lobed, not webbed like waterfowl
- head bobs pigeon-like while swimming

Sora
Porzana carolina

- WS: 14 inches
- found in marshy habitats
- heard more often than seen; call a long, high, descending whinny.
- breeding adults have gray breast and black face

Killdeer
Charadrius vociferus

- WS: 24 inches
- black neck bands and red eye-ring
- orange rump seen in flight

Long-billed Curlew
Numenius americanus

- WS: 35 inches
- bill extremely long and down turned
- found in open meadows
- calls *curlew* in flight

Greater Yellowlegs
Tringa melanoleuca

- WS: 28 inches
- commonly wades in shallow water
- bill slightly up turned

Spotted Sandpiper
Actitis macularia

- WS: 15 inches
- distinct spotted breast
- bobs up and down frequently

Wilson's Snipe
Gallinago delicata

- WS: 18 inches
- stout body with a long, blunt bill
- dark stripes along head and back
- very secretive (more common to hear during aerial courtship displays than it is to see in the open)
- call a loud *tuk tuk tuk*; also a rising whinny
- typically found in wetlands and mudflats

Wilson's Phalarope
Phalaropus tricolor

- WS: 17 inches
- unlike most birds, the female of this species (and other phalaropes) is more colorful and distinct than the male
- can be found wading or swimming (often spinning in tight circles) in wetland habitats

Gull (Laridae) Family

Franklin's Gull
Larus pipixcan

- WS: 36 inches
- breeding adults have dark head, reddish bill, and white markings above and below eye
- less common in GYE than ring-billed and California gulls

Ring-billed Gull
Larus delawarensis

- WS: 48 inches
- dark ring around end of bill and small size distinguish ring-billed from California gulls
- common within GYE and widespread throughout North America

California Gull
Larus californicus

- WS: 54 inches
- breeding adults have white heads like ring-billed gulls, but bill is longer with both red and black markings at tip

Vulture (Cathartidae) Family

Turkey Vulture
Cathartes aura

- WS: 67 inches
- dark-feathered body and bare red head are unlike any other bird
- soar in a strong dihedral (V-shape), often rocking back and forth (unlike the steady soaring of eagles)
- exclusive scavengers; found either searching for carrion or on a carcass

Eagle & Hawk (Accipitridae) Family
Eagles

Both of North America's eagles can be found in this region, with bald eagles seen more frequently. These two species of eagles are excellent soarers and have strong, steady wingbeats in flight.

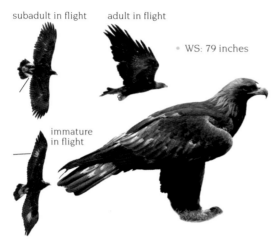

subadult in flight   adult in flight

• WS: 79 inches

immature in flight

Golden Eagle
Aquila chrysaetos

Golden eagles are more predatory and less scavenging than the more common bald eagle. These hunters are capable of taking large prey such as young deer and bighorn sheep. When perched, the best field mark is their golden nape. In flight, an adult's underwing and head will appear uniformly dark, but juveniles (and some subadults) will have clear white patches underwing. Present year-round.

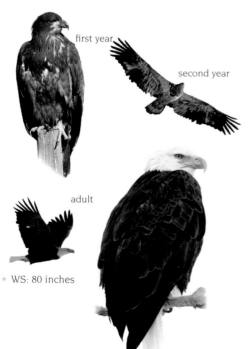

first year

second year

adult

• WS: 80 inches

Bald Eagle
Haliaeetus leucocephalus

Bald eagles have made a remarkable comeback since the last half of the twentieth century when their low numbers placed them on the endangered species list. Now it is common to see our national symbol along rivers and lakes throughout the region any time of year. At a distance both species of eagle can look similar, but once the white head, white tail, and dark body can be seen, an adult bald eagle is unmistakable. Bald eagles take several years to mature and mottled juveniles are often confused for golden eagles. A juvenile bald eagle has much more random white streaks underwing compared to a juvenile golden eagle.

Harrier

Northern Harrier
Circus cyaneus

This medium-sized raptor can often be found hunting low to the ground above grasslands, sage flats, and marshes with its wings held in dihedral (V-shape). Males are gray above and light below, females are brown, and juveniles are rust colored. All forms exhibit an obvious white rump above the tail.

- WS: 43 inches

juvenile

female from behind

Accipiters

Sharp-shinned Hawk
Accipiter striatus

Sharp-shinned hawks are the smallest of the accipiters and very difficult to discern from a Cooper's hawk. In flight, the head is proportionally smaller and the leading edge of the wing is more S-shaped.

- WS: 23 inches

Cooper's Hawk
Accipiter cooperii

When perched, the back of the head of a Cooper's hawk may appear more square than the sharp-shinned; head is proportionally larger in flight. Females are 20 to 30 percent larger than males (as in other accipiters); juveniles are similar to adults in size, but with vertical (not horizontal) streaking along the breast.

- WS: 31 inches

Northern Goshawk
Accipiter gentilis

The largest of all North American accipiters, the goshawk is capable of pursuing other birds in flight as well as small mammals. The adult's blood-red eye and eye-stripe are diagnostic, but juveniles closely resemble Cooper's hawks.

- WS: 41 inches

juvenile

Buteos

These raptors are the hawks of open spaces. They are all excellent soaring predators and usually hunt from hundreds of feet above the ground. All the buteos of the GYE exhibit plumage polymorphism, which means that plumage may be dark or light. In the GYE, lighter plumages are much more common.

Red-tailed Hawk
Buteo jamaicensis

• WS: 49 inches

juvenile

light adult

dark adult

Red-tailed hawks vary considerably in plumages, so knowing several field marks is important. Tail color is not always visible (and juveniles don't have a red tail); look instead for the belly band on a perched bird or the dark patagium (narrow marking on the leading edge of the wing) in flight.

Rough-legged Hawk
Buteo lagopus

• WS: 53 inches

Rough-legged hawks are winter visitors to this region and are the most commonly seen hawk from December through March. In flight, the dark rectangular marking on the forewings is distinctive.

Swainson's Hawk
Buteo swainsoni

• WS: 51 inches

Swainson's hawks have a two-toned coloration underwing and a small patch of white plumage under the chin. In flight they appear more delicate than other buteos and their wings may have a subtle dihedral (V-shape) while soaring.

Ferruginous Hawk
Buteo regalis

• WS: 56 inches

This is the least encountered buteo of the region; more commonly found in the open plains outside of the ecosystem. From underneath, the clean, unmarked tail and dark feathers of the legs are both unique to this species.

Osprey

Osprey
Pandion haliaetus

Osprey specialize in preying upon fish and are typically seen along lakes and rivers. Its long wings are usually bent slightly, and the eye-stripe and light breast distinguish the osprey from bald eagles. They migrate as far as South America during winter.

• WS: 63 inches

Falcon (Falconidae) Family

American Kestrel
Falco sparverius

Kestrels are the smallest North American falcon, often seen perched on telephone wires or hovering in midair while searching for prey. Males are very colorful; females have similar markings but less color. Kestrels typically nest in cavities excavated by woodpeckers.

• WS: 22 inches

Peregrine Falcon
Falco peregrinus

Generally considered to be the fastest animal in the world, the peregrine falcon is capable of diving at up to 200 miles per hour. Peregrines, like osprey, can be found on six continents and migrate long distances. The distinct hood and short, slender wings are good field marks.

• WS: 41 inches

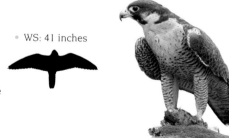

Prairie Falcon
Falco mexicanus

The prairie falcon is very similar in size and shape to the peregrine falcon. Look for the narrow "mustache" marking on a perched bird or for dark "armpits" on a prairie falcon in flight.

• WS: 40 inches

Grouse (Phasianidae) Family

The members of this group of chunky birds are very capable of prolonged flight but often choose to walk instead. From the drumming wingbeats of the ruffed grouse to the spectacular displays of the sage grouse, the courtship behaviors of these birds are a dramatic part of the spring wildlife experience. Each of these grouse species can be seen any time of year in the GYE.

Greater Sage Grouse
Centrocercus urophasianus

- WS: 36 inches
- females brown bodied; both males and females have black bellies
- strongly prefer open sagebrush habitats
- male courtship displays are elaborate and accompanied by loud, almost robotic vocalizations

male displaying

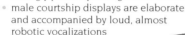

male displaying

Dusky Grouse
Dendragapus obscurus

- WS: 26 inches
- long tail with gray tips
- females brown bodied, speckled white
- previously called blue grouse

Ruffed Grouse
Bonasa umbellus

- WS: 22 inches
- distinct crest often visible
- commonly heard "drumming" during spring (a thumping sound made by beating wings)

Pigeons & Dove (Columbidae) Family

Rock Pigeon
Columba livia

- WS: 28 inches
- plumage varies widely in color and pattern
- native to Europe

Mourning Dove
Zenaida macroura

- WS: 18 inches
- very slender bodied and long, pointed tail

Eurasian Collared Dove
Streptopelia decaocto

- WS: 22 inches
- dark wing tips and square tails
- native to Europe

Owl (Strigidae) Family

Short-eared Owl
Asio flammeus

- WS: 38 inches
- short ear tufts may not be visible
- sexes similar, but males slightly paler
- yellow eyes surrounded by dark patches

Long-eared Owl
Asio otus

- WS: 36 inches
- long ear tufts and rufous-colored facial disk
- similar features as great horned owl but smaller

Great Horned Owl
Bubo virginianus

- WS: 44 inches
- most common large owl in GYE; widespread
- preys on a diversity of small mammals
- classic hooting call often matches the cadence of the phrase, *who's awake, me too*

Great Gray Owl
Strix nebulosa

- WS: 52 inches
- GYE's largest (but not heaviest) owl
- very large facial disk with no ear tufts
- the GYE is one of the best places in the United States to see this owl

Burrowing Owl
Athene cunicularia

- WS: 21 inches
- much longer legs proportionally than any other owl
- pale "eyebrows"
- nests underground in open sagebrush and grasslands

Northern Pygmy-Owl
Glaucidium gnoma

- WS: 12 inches
- spotted head and sides
- back of head has eyespots
- preys upon small birds, often during daytime

Northern Saw-whet Owl
Aegolius acadicus

- WS: 17 inches
- very similar to the slightly larger boreal owl, but with darker bill and more consistent brown streaking across breast
- call is a repetitive series of high-pitched hoots

Boreal Owl
Aegolius funereus

- WS: 21 inches
- breast can be streaked or spotted
- both saw-whet and boreal owls found in conifer forests
- paler bill than saw-whet owl

Nighthawks & Swifts

Common Nighthawk
Caprimulgidae Family
Chordeiles minor

- WS: 24 inches
- white bar near tips of long wings seen in flight
- active at night but seen (and heard) at dusk hunting insects
- listen for buzzing *hoovvv* of male's display dive

White-throated Swift
Apodidae Family
Aeronautes saxatalis

- WS: 15 inches
- extremely fast and often found near cliffs
- slightly forked tail
- white chest and throat

Hummingbird (Trochilidae) Family

Calliope Hummingbird
Stellula calliope

- WS: 4.25 inches
- males unmistakable with purple iridescent streaks on throat.
- females have subtle spots along throat
- when perched, wing tips extend to tip of tail or slightly beyond
- smallest bird in North America

Broad-tailed Hummingbird
Selasphorus platycercus

- WS: 5.25 inches
- male has iridescent, rose-colored throat
- when perched, wing tips don't reach end of tail

Rufous Hummingbird
Selasphorus rufus

- WS: 4.5 inches
- male has orange head and back with dark maroon throat
- female has small dark patch in the center of otherwise pale throat

Kingfisher (Alcedinidae) Family

Belted Kingfisher
Ceryle alcyon

♀   ♂

- WS: 20 inches
- tufted crest, dagger-like bill, and band across chest distinguish kingfishers from any other bird
- female has maroon band across belly
- skilled fishers, always found near water

Woodpecker (Picidae) Family

Lewis's Woodpecker
Melanerpes lewis

- WS: 21 inches
- dark appearance overall
- red face and dark black or iridescent green back
- not as commonly seen as other woodpeckers in GYE
- males and females look identical

Northern Flicker
Colaptes auratus

♂

- WS: 20 inches
- large size, black bib, and spotted chest noticeable when perched or feeding on the ground
- in flight, white rump and red wings visible
- females lack red "mustache" streak

Downy Woodpecker
Picoides pubescens

♂

- WS: 12 inches
- like hairy woodpeckers, downys have white "backpack"
- distinct tuft of feathers at base of bill

Hairy Woodpecker
Picoides villosus

♀

 ♂

- WS: 15 inches
- larger than downy woodpecker and proportionally longer bill
- males of both hairy and downy woodpeckers have red nape

Red-naped Sapsucker
Sphyrapicus nuchalis

♂

- WS: 16 inches
- red crown and throat
- white sides and barring on back
- females similar but often with white chin
- drill shallow horizontal rows that they drink sap from or trap insects in

Flycatcher (Tyrannidae) Family

Eastern Kingbird
Tyrannus tyrannus

- WS: 15 inches
- dark crown and back
- white or light-gray breast
- white band along tip of tail can be seen in flight or while perched

Western Kingbird
Tyrannus verticalis

- WS: 15 inches
- gray head, dark wings and tail
- light-gray breast fading to a light-yellow belly

Dusky Flycatcher
Empidonax oberholseri

- WS: 8 inches
- the *Empidonax* group of flycatchers are notoriously difficult to distinguish, and the following four species can be found in the GYE: dusky (most common), Hammond's, willow, and cordilleran
- dusky and Hammond's are the most similar, but Hammond's tends to be found at the top of tall conifers, while dusky prefers low shrubs
- vocalizations are usually needed for certain identification

---

Lark (Alaudidae) Family

Horned Lark
Eremophila alpestris

- WS: 12 inches
- tends to occur in flocks; more common in late winter and early spring
- dark mask and pale yellow throat more distinct in males but also present in females

---

Swallow (Hirundinidae) Family

Tree Swallow
Tachycineta bicolor

- WS: 14.5 inches
- iridescent blue-green back with white breast and belly
- nests in cavities and birdhouses

Violet-green Swallow
Tachycineta thalassina

- WS: 13.5 inches
- iridescent green and purple back with white breast and belly
- white face extends above eye

Bank Swallow
Riparia riparia

- WS: 13 inches
- dull gray coloration with band across breast
- nests in riverbanks and lakeshores

Cliff Swallow
Petrochelidon pyrrhonota

- WS: 13.5 inches
- pale forehead is only found on this swallow species
- nests are constructed from mud and found in rocky areas

Barn Swallow
Hirundo rustica

- WS: 15 inches
- GYE's only fork-tailed swallow
- dark blue back, light orange belly, and dark orange neck and forehead
- female coloration similar but lighter orange belly and shorter tail
- nests constructed from mud and found in cliffs or on buildings

Chickadee (Paridae) Family

Black-capped Chickadee
Poecile atricapillus

- WS: 8 inches
- common year-round
- slightly smaller than mountain chickadee
- vocalizes frequently *chickadee-dee-dee*

Mountain Chickadee
Poecile gambeli

- WS: 8.5 inches
- white stripe above eye distinguishes mountain from black-capped chickadee

Jay, Raven, & Crow (Corvidae) Family

All species in this group are highly intelligent and vocalize frequently. These birds can be found throughout the ecosystem, but the Steller's jay and gray jay prefer forested habitats.

Common Raven
Corvus corax

- WS: 53 inches
- larger than crows with thicker bill and wedge-shaped tail in flight
- as scavengers, ravens are often associated with carrion

American Crow
Corvus brachyrhynchos

- WS: 39 inches
- more slender bill and squared tail in flight distinguish crows from ravens
- seen more in urban areas than ravens

Black-billed Magpie
Pica hudsonia

- WS: 25 inches
- common year-round
- long tail and unique black and white markings unlike any other bird species

Gray Jay
Perisoreus canadensis

- WS: 18 inches
- nicknamed "camp-robber" due to its tendency to beg at campsites

Clark's Nutcracker
Nucifraga columbiana

- WS: 24 inches
- dark wings and very sharp bill
- harsh cry heard frequently within their coniferous habitat
- favors seeds of whitebark pines, which it caches by the thousands

Steller's Jay
Cyanocitta stelleri

- WS: 19 inches
- dark head and deep blue body with distinct crest
- white eyebrow often visible
- like other jays, is adept at mimicking other birds, including the screech of a red-tailed hawk

Creeper (Certhidae) Family

Brown Creeper
Certhia americana

- WS: 8 inches
- often seen gleaning vertically on conifer trees
- streaked brown back is excellent camouflage against tree bark
- curved bill

Nuthatch (Sittidae) Family

Red-breasted Nuthatch
Sitta canadensis

- WS: 8.5 inches
- black eye-stripe and reddish breast distinguish it from the less frequently seen white-breasted nuthatch

White-breasted Nuthatch
Sitta carolinensis

- WS: 11 inches
- white face without red breast and dark eye-stripe
- less common than red-breasted nuthatch

Wren (Troglodytidae) Family

House Wren
Troglodytes aedon

- WS: 6 inches
- brown overall with obvious barring on wings and tail
- nests in cavities and birdhouses
- loud warbling song heard in spring and early summer

Kinglet (Regulidae) Family

Golden-crowned Kinglet
Regulus satrapa

- WS: 7 inches
- gray with light yellow wings and striped face
- yellow crown
- both kinglet species can be found in conifer forests, often high in the canopy

Ruby-crowned Kinglet
Regulus calendula

- WS: 7.5 inches
- gray and olive, with wing-bars and red crown

Thrush (Turdidae) Family

Mountain Bluebird
Sialia currucoides

- WS: 14 inches
- males are vibrant blue and females are mostly gray with light blue wings
- nest in cavities and bluebird boxes, usually in open meadows
- Idaho state bird

Townsend's Solitaire
Myadestes townsendi

- WS: 14.5 inches
- gray with white eye-ring and light orange marking on wings
- found in conifer forests

Hermit Thrush
Catharus guttatus

- WS: 11.5 inches
- brown with spotted breast, white eye-ring, and rufous tail
- loud flute-like song heard frequently in spring and summer

American Robin
Turdus migratorius

- WS: 17 inches
- gray backed with obvious orange breast and partial eye-ring
- commonly seen and heard in residential areas

Shrike (Laniidae) Family

Northern Shrike
Lanius excubitor

- WS: 15 inches
- gray back, black mask, and dark wings
- preys upon small rodents and insects as the hooked bill suggests
- breeds in arctic but migrates into the GYE during winter
- nickname is "butcher bird" due to its predatory nature and habit of impaling prey on thorny shrubs

Mimic Thrush (Mimidae) Family

Gray Catbird
Dumetella carolinensis

- WS: 11 inches
- dark gray body, black cap, and reddish undertail coverts
- call is raspy *meow* like a cat

Sage Thrasher
Oreoscoptes montanus

- WS: 12 inches
- obvious streaking on breast
- found in sagebrush habitat

American Pipit
Motacillidae Family
Anthus rubescens

- WS: 10.5 inches
- streaked breast with faint eye-stripe
- frequently bobs tail
- can be found at all elevations including above treeline

American Dipper
Cinclidae Family
Cinclus mexicanus

- WS: 11 inches
- mostly gray with short tail
- frequently found in fast-moving water and seen swimming underwater in pursuit of aquatic invertebrates

Waxwing (Bombycillidae) Family

Bohemian Waxwing
Bombycilla garrulus

- WS: 14 inches
- black mask and yellow-tipped tail
- yellow-streaked wing and less white surrounding eye differentiates from cedar waxwing

Cedar Waxwing
Bombycilla cedrorum

- WS: 12 inches
- breast is more brown with yellowish belly compared with bohemian waxwing
- typically seen in flocks; more common in winter

Starling (Sturnidae) Family

European Starling
Sturnus vulgaris

- WS: 16 inches
- streaked breast and short tail
- intoduced from Europe and often found in residential areas
- frequently in large flocks

Vireo (Vireonidae) Family

Warbling Vireo
Vireo gilvus

- WS: 8.5 inches
- olive-brown overall with dark crown and lighter eye-stripe
- typically found in aspen or conifer forests

Warbler & Sparrow (Emberizidae) Family

Yellow-rumped Warbler
Dendroica coronata

- WS: 9 inches
- yellow flanks, throat, and rump seen on both males and females
- males also have yellow crown and more slate-blue overall

Yellow Warbler
Dendroica petechia

- WS: 8 inches
- males and females both yellow bodied
- males have red streaks on breast

MacGillivray's Warbler
Oporornis tolmiei

- WS: 7.5 inches
- males and females both have gray head, olive wings, and partial eye-ring
- males have darker head

Wilson's Warbler
Wilsonia pusilla

- WS: 7 inches
- males and females have similar coloration, but females lack distinct black crown
- often found in willow habitats

Common Yellowthroat
Geothlypis trichas

- WS: 7 inches
- males and females both have yellow throat, yellow undertail coverts, and olive-yellow back and wings
- males have distinct black mask with white stripe across forehead
- commonly heard during spring and summer, song is *witchity-witchity-witchity*
- frequents willow habitats

Black-headed Grosbeak
Pheucticus melanocephalus

- WS: 12 inches
- very thick bill is bi-colored (dark gray above and lighter below) in both males and females
- stocky with large head ♀

♂

Lazuli Bunting
Passerina amoena

- WS: 9 inches
- male is vibrant blue with orange band on breast
- female is dull gray overall with pale wing-bars
- males and females both have thick finch-like bill

♂

Green-tailed Towhee
Pipilo chlorurus

- WS: 10 inches
- males and females identical with rufous crown, white neck, and olive-green wings and tail

Vesper Sparrow
Pooecetes gramineus

- WS: 10 inches
- pale belly and streaked back with white eye-ring
- in flight, outer tail feathers white
- longer tail than savannah sparrow

Savannah Sparrow
Passerculus sandwichensis

- WS: 7 inches
- subtle yellow eye-stripe with streaked breast
- notched tail

Song Sparrow
Melospiza melodia

- WS: 8 inches
- commonly seen and heard
- dark central spot on breast surrounded by streaking

Lark Sparrow
Chondestes grammacus

- WS: 11 inches
- rufous cheek and crown
- white breast with dark central spot
- uncommon

American Tree Sparrow
Spizella arborea

- WS: 10 inches
- rufous crown, dark eye-line, and dark central spot on breast
- bill is dark above and light below

Chipping Sparrow
Spizella passerina

- WS: 8.5 inches
- reddish crown and dark eye-stripe
- light breast with no central spot

Dark-eyed Junco
Junco hyemalis

- WS: 9 inches
- there are several variations within this species, but all have dark or gray head, dark eyes, and white outer tail feathers

Oregon form

gray-headed form

White-crowned Sparrow
Zonotrichia leucophrys

- WS: 10 inches
- pale breast with white eye-line and dark crown
- pink bill

Fox Sparrow
Passerella iliaca

- WS: 10.5 inches
- gray head and streaked breast with yellow bill

Snow Bunting
Plectrophenax nivalis

- WS: 14 inches
- breeds in arctic regions but found in GYE during winter, often seen in flocks

winter

♂

Blackbird (Icteridae) Family

Bobolink
Dolichonyx oryzivorus

- WS: 11 inches
- males dark with ivory or light yellow nape
- females drab with dark crown

♂

Western Meadowlark
Sturnella neglecta

- WS: 15 inches
- bright yellow breast with black "bib"
- beautiful song heard in sage habitats
- state bird of both Montana and Wyoming

Yellow-headed Blackbird
Xanthocephalus xanthocephalus

- WS: 15 inches
- males with bright yellow head, dark body with white wing-bars
- females brown overall with light-yellow breast and head

Red-winged Blackbird
Agelaius phoeniceus

- WS: 13 inches
- male all black with obvious red and yellow patches on wings
- female drab with strongly streaked breast

Bullock's Oriole
Icterus bullockii

- WS: 12 inches
- male has bright orange breast and face with black crown and dark wings with white markings
- female has yellow head and breast with white-streaked wings

Brewer's Blackbird
Euphagus cyanocephalus

- WS: 15 inches
- males slightly iridescent green-violet with bright yellow eye

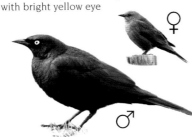

Brown-headed Cowbird
Molothrus ater

- WS: 12 inches
- males have brown head and iridescent blue body
- often found in association with cows or bison

Western Tanager
Thraupidae Family
Piranga ludoviciana

- WS: 11.5 inches
- males have brilliant red-orange face, yellow breast and nape, and black wings

Finch (Fringillidae) Family

Pine Siskin
Carduelis pinus

- WS: 9 inches
- brown with streaked breast and yellow-fringed wings
- relatively thin bill
- frequents conifer forests

American Goldfinch
Carduelis tristis

- WS: 9 inches
- male is bright yellow with black wings and black forehead
- female is dull yellow with more distinct wing-bars

Pine Grosbeak
Pinicola enucleator

- WS: 14.5 inches
- male with dark-red head, breast, and back, otherwise gray bodied
- female with yellow head, breast, and back, but still has two distinct white wing-bars
- found in conifer forests

White-winged Crossbill
Loxia leucoptera

- WS: 10.5 inches
- male and female both have more distinct white wing-bars than red crossbill
- bill size varies in this genus, but all are specialized for extracting seeds from conifers

Red Crossbill
Loxia curvirostra

- WS: 11 inches
- male reddish with dark wings and subtle wing-bars
- female yellow bodied with no wing-bars

Gray-crowned Rosy Finch
Leucosticte tephocotis

- WS: 13 inches
- dark brown breast with gray cheeks, dark throat, and dark bill (yellow bill seen in its first winter)
- rose-colored streaked wings seen in all plumages

Cassin's Finch
Carpodacus cassinii

- WS: 11.5 inches
- male has faint red breast with crown more red than other areas
- female drab brown with strongly streaked breast
- more likely to be found in high conifer forest than house finch

House Finch
Carpodacus mexicanus

- WS: 9.5 inches
- male is brown bodied with bright red neck and crown
- streaked sides unlike Cassin's finch

Evening Grosbeak
Coccothraustes vespertinus

- WS: 14 inches
- male with distinct yellow eyebrow and dark wing
- females lack yellow eyebrow but have dark wings and more subtle yellow coloration

House Sparrow
Passeridae Family
Passer domesticus

- WS: 9 inches
- males have dark throat, rufous neck, and white stripe on wings
- females more drab with yellow bill
- introduced into North America in the late 1800s and has become one of the most common birds on the continent
- often associated with urban areas and human development

Mammals

The Greater Yellowstone Ecosystem is famous in part for the presence of rare and charismatic species such as gray wolves, grizzly bears, lynx, and wolverines. This section of the *Field Guide* covers those "celebrity" species as well as many other fascinating mammals that call the GYE home.

All mammals share certain characteristics: the presence of hair at some stage in life, the nursing of young, and warm-bloodedness (the ability to maintain a fairly constant body temperature). Despite these similarities, each species has its own distinct physical attributes, habitat preferences, and vocalizations.

The three main types of hair or fur that mammals grow are whiskers (vibrissae), underhair, and guard hair. Underhair is closest to the skin and usually soft. Guard hair is more external, coarser, and hollow, allowing it to trap air for additional insulation. Such fur plays a critical role in cold regions like the GYE. Most species grow a much thicker coat for winter, and fur color changes seasonally in some species such as long-tailed weasel and snowshoe hare. White fur against a snowy backdrop provides excellent camouflage.

Mammals employ a variety of strategies for survival during winter. Migrations are more typically associated with birds, but many mammals also migrate over shorter distances. Large mammals like bison, bighorn sheep, and elk migrate from higher elevations during summer to winter ranges at lower elevations. This is why we see thousands of elk in low-elevation locations like Jackson Hole's National Elk Refuge in mid-winter and none during summer. Hibernation is another remarkable strategy for coping with cold temperatures and limited food availability. Several rodents endure deep hibernations that can last up to seven months. Bears are not considered true hibernators, but nevertheless den up and lower their metabolic rate substantially during the winter months.

Most mammals instinctively time mating and giving birth so that young are born in late spring or early summer when food is abundant. Gestation varies widely; the longest is bison (about nine months), while small rodents such as squirrels, chipmunks, and ground squirrels have gestation periods of just 25 to 35 days. Members of the weasel and bear families use a strategy of delayed implantation. Fertilization occurs after mating, but the embryo development pauses until later in the year. This allows bears, for example, to give birth in mid-winter within the security of their dens. Also, mothers can abort the embryo if they sense that they won't be able to provide sufficient nourishment to their newborns. Mountain lions are unusual in that they will mate and give birth any time of year.

Some mammal species are relatively easy to observe, while others are nearly impossible to see in the wild. The best way to find wildlife is to know what habitat type they prefer, which is based largely on what they eat. All mammals can be categorized by diet: herbivores (strict plant-eaters), carnivores (meat-eaters), and omnivores (plant- and meat-eaters). These categories can be further split. Herbivores that primarily forage on shrubs are browsers; those that mainly eat grass are grazers.

Carnivores tend to be either scavengers or predators. A predator such as a gray wolf prefers to kill its food, while coyotes are as likely to scavenge a meal from a carcass. The purest carnivores are the various cat and weasel species. Bears are the quintessential omnivores, willing to sample just about anything.

The largest terrestrial mammals in the region (and the world) are herbivores, which include all the hoofed mammals, beavers, and many species of rodents. All of the GYE's ungulates (hoofed mammals) are ruminants, which means that they have a stomach with four compartments capable of digesting plant cellulose into energy. The animal briefly chews and swallows plant material into its first chamber, the rumen, and then later regurgitates the material and additional saliva (collectively called "cud") to again chew it more slowly, further breaking down the cellulose.

In addition to understanding an animal's habitat and dietary preferences, wildlife watchers should also know what time of day or night a species is most active. Some mammals, such as pronghorn and bison, are active throughout the day (diurnal), while others, such as flying squirrels and bats, are active only at night (nocturnal). The vast majority of mammals fall into the category of crepuscular, which means that they are most active at dusk and dawn. During the heat of summer, these windows of lower temperatures are the best times to see many species such as elk, moose, beavers, wolves, coyotes, and bears.

As someone who guides people throughout this region, I strongly recommend spending time with a park ranger or qualified naturalist guide. Our extensive time spent in these parks gives us insight into the most likely locations to find wildlife, and we're glad to share the fascinating stories that reveal the amazing lives behind each species. Many organizations offer this service, but before you sign up, always ask about a potential guide's experience in the GYE and whether they have a natural science background.

Seeing a large mammal in the wild is always a highlight of any visit to a national park. Unfortunately, such excitement sometimes leads to human behavior that is disrespectful to wildlife. The National Park Service enforces a policy requiring people to stay at least 25 yards from animals such as bison, moose, and elk, and at least 100 yards from bears and wolves. Regardless of distance, if your presence is affecting the animal's behavior in any way, you are too close. Quality binoculars and a telephoto lens enable viewing from a safe and respectful distance. Finally, feeding wild animals is never a good idea. Some foods are themselves harmful, and habituating a wild animal to human handouts—intentionally or by leaving food unattended—always leads to unhappy outcomes, most often for the animal. Remember: "A fed bear is a dead bear!" Please do your part to protect the wildlife you enjoy.

Bat (Chiroptera) Order

Bats are the only mammals capable of true flight. They feed nocturnally, using echo-location to avoid obstacles and find prey. During winter, bats either migrate or hibernate in colonies. More species of bats occur in tropical regions than temperate zones. The four species below are the most common in the GYE. All of these bats are very difficult to distinguish in flight; they are most likely to be seen hunting insects near water.

Silver-haired Bat
Lasionycteris noctivagans

- length: 3.5 to 4.5 inches
- weight: 0.3 ounce
- silver-tipped hair on back and longer ears than other bats
- often solitary

Long-legged Myotis
Myotis evotis

- length: 3.5 inches
- weight: 0.25 ounce
- slightly smaller than other bats; fur on back is reddish brown

Little Brown Myotis
Myotis lucifugus

- length: 3.5 inches
- weight: 0.25 ounce
- most common bat in GYE
- small nose and large ears

Big Brown Bat
Eptesicus fuscus

- length: 4 to 5 inches
- weight: 0.4 ounce
- larger than other bats in GYE

Shrew (Insectivora) Order

Masked Shrew
Sorex cinereus

- length: 3 to 4 inches with tail
- weight: 0.2 ounce
- resemble rodents but are not closely related
- primarily preys upon insects and other invertebrates
- often found in marshy areas

Rodent (Rodentia) Order

This group of animals is a critical food base for many predators. Several of these species remain active year-round (red squirrel, muskrat, beaver, and porcupine), while others cope with winter by hibernating for up to seven months of the year (ground squirrels and marmots).

Deer Mouse
Peromyscus maniculatus

- length with tail: 5 to 7 inches
- weight: ~1 ounce
- large ears, long tail is bi-colored (brown above and light below)

Montane Vole
Microtus montanus

Red-backed vole for comparison

- length with tail: 5 to 8 inches
- weight: 1 to 3 ounces
- small ears, dark gray coloration, and small eyes
- difficult to distinguish from other vole species

Least Chipmunk
Tamias minimus

- length with tail: 7 to 8 inches
- weight: 1 to 2 ounces
- smallest and most common chipmunk in GYE

Golden-mantled Ground Squirrel
Spermophilus lateralis

- length with tail: 8 to 12 inches
- weight: 8 to 10 ounces
- commonly confused with chipmunks, but side stripes don't extend through face
- begs frequently (please don't feed)

Northern Pocket Gopher
Thomomys talpoides

- length with tail: 8 to 12 inches
- weight: 3 to 4 ounces
- rare to see above ground, but remnant soil tubes indicate activity

Red Squirrel
Tamiasciurus hudsonicus

- length with tail: 11 to 14 inches
- weight: 7 to 8 ounces
- reddish brown with distinct bushy tail
- common in conifer forests
- frequently chatters when disturbed
- signs of red squirrel activity include large "middens" of stored pine cones

Uinta Ground Squirrel
Spermophilus armatus

young ground squirrel

These light-brown squirrels are ubiquitous in the GYE. They live socially underground and so are commonly mistaken for prairie dogs. Ground squirrels typically hibernate from August through late March and are an important food source for many predators including grizzly bears, badgers, coyotes, and several raptor species. When alarmed, ground squirrels vocalize with a high-pitched stuttering whistle.

• length with tail: 11 to 14 inches
• weight: 7 to 13 ounces

Black-tailed Prairie Dog
Cynomys ludovicianus

As this rodent's name suggests, the tip (usually the last third) of its tail is black. Prairie dogs are usually found in large colonies, also called towns. They occur outside the GYE (to the east in Wyoming and Montana), but are included here as a comparison to the much more common Uinta ground squirrel.

• length with tail: 12 to 14 inches
• weight: 1.5 to 2.5 pounds

Yellow-bellied Marmot
Marmota flaviventris

Marmots prefer rocky slopes where they can be found sunbathing or foraging. Some individuals are almost black in color. Marmots emit a high-pitched, single, whistling call when potential danger is nearby.

• length with tail: 1.5 to 2.5 feet
• weight: 5 to 10 pounds

Porcupine
Erethizon dorsatum

Porcupines are a truly remarkable species with a fascinating natural history. While most rodents have extremely high reproductive rates, porcupines usually give birth to just one pup every year. They compensate for this by having a low mortality rate, which is primarily due to their infamous quills. An adult's entire back and tail are covered with as many as 30,000 of these specialized, barbed hairs, an excellent deterrent against predators. These quills readily impale any attacker, but, contrary to folklore, cannot be "thrown."

- length with tail: 2.5 to 4.5 feet
- weight: 10 to 40 pounds

Muskrat
Ondatra zibethicus

Muskrats are aquatic rodents that are primarily vegetarian, but they occasionally eat crayfish and salamanders. Due to similarities in habitat, muskrats are occasionally misidentified as small beavers. Muskrats are much smaller and have a vertically flattened, narrow tail that serves as a rudder while swimming.

- length with tail: 18 to 26 inches
- weight: 2 to 4 pounds

Beaver
Castor canadensis

Beavers are the largest rodent in North America. Unique adaptations include sharp incisors, waterproof fur, wide flattened tail, and webbed feet. Impressive architects, beavers reshape the landscape by felling trees and building dams, canals, and lodges. A beaver pond is typically home to a colony of up to eight related individuals. In the 1800s demand for their luxuriant, waterproof fur drove early explorers to this region. Nearly exterminated, beaver populations are fully recovered.

- length with tail: 35 to 45 inches
- weight: 30 to 90 pounds

Northern Flying Squirrel
Glaucomys sabrinus

- length with tail: 10 to 12 inches
- weight: 5 ounces
- very nocturnal and rarely seen
- large dark eyes
- capable of gliding from tree to tree

Rabbit, Hare, and Pika (Lagomorpha) Order

Snowshoe Hare
Lepus americanus

- length with tail: 15 to 20 inches
- weight: 2 to 4 pounds
- huge rear feet
- fur is white in winter
- tracks much more common to see than animal itself

winter

summer

White-tailed Jackrabbit
Lepus townsendii

- length with tail: 23 to 29 inches
- weight: 6 to 9 pounds
- extremely large ears
- like snowshoe hares, fur is white in winter
- non-social and exclusively vegetarian

Pika
Ochotona princeps

- length: 7 to 9 inches
- weight: 4 to 6 ounces
- short ears and short tail
- found on rocky slopes; active year-round

Antlers vs. Horns

These two terms are commonly interchanged to describe the durable material protruding from the heads of hoofed mammals. Their purpose is often the same (combating one another in pursuit of females), but they are very different structures.

Horns

The main distinction that can be made between antlers and horns is the material that they are made out of. Horns are made out of fibrous keratin (just like hair and fingernails), are worn by both males and females, and are usually never shed. The males of both pronghorn and bighorn sheep carry much larger horns than females, which can be helpful in distinguishing gender. Pronghorn do have true horns, but they are unique in that the horn's dark sheath is shed each year after the rut. Bighorn sheep rams grow their horns throughout their lives, and, unlike other animals, their age can be estimated based on the prominant ridges every several inches along the horn. The arrows below indicate two of these ridges; the span between represents one year of growth.

Pronghorn Horn

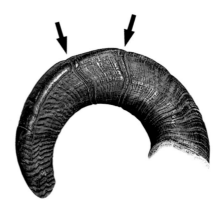

Bighorn Sheep Horn

Bison Horn

Antlers

Mammals within the deer family have antlers rather than horns. Antlers are specialized bone structures that grow from a permanent part of the skull called the pedicle. They are grown and shed each year and are worn only by males. Of course, there are exceptions to every tendency in nature. Caribou, which are not found within this ecosystem, break the rule: females also grow antlers.

Annual antler growth by moose, elk, and deer is truly a phenomenal process. Each winter, the males drop their antlers and begin growing a new pair in late winter or early spring. Most of this growth occurs during summer, when velvet covers the antlers (image at right). As summer comes to a close, the testosterone levels of the males increases, and the velvet dies and is shed or rubbed off. At this point, the antlers are ready to serve their primary purpose as the animal's weapon during battles with other males as part of the autumn courtship of females.

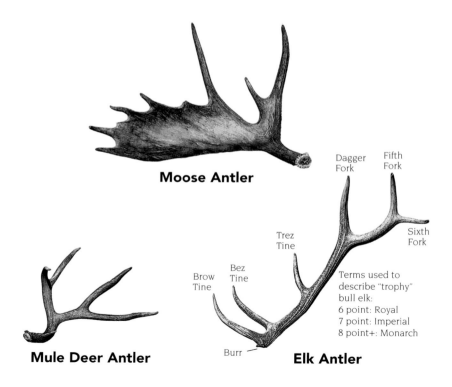

Moose Antler

Dagger Fork

Fifth Fork

Trez Tine

Sixth Fork

Brow Tine

Bez Tine

Terms used to describe "trophy" bull elk:
6 point: Royal
7 point: Imperial
8 point+: Monarch

Mule Deer Antler

Burr

Elk Antler

Bovidae Family

Mountain Goat
Oreamnos americanus

This region's scattered populations of mountain goats are specialized for vertical terrain. Both males (billies) and females (nannies) have 8- to 12-inch horns, but the males' are thicker at the base and arc backward more smoothly than on females. Babies (called kids) are born in late spring and navigate steep cliffs within hours of being born. Mountain goats are not native to the GYE and were introduced here in the 1940s and 1950s.

- shoulder height: 36 to 42 inches
- weight: 100 to 300 pounds

Bighorn Sheep
Ovis canadensis

As the name of this animal implies, the horns of bighorn sheep are a critical component of their natural history and identification. Males (rams) grow horns that will eventually curl 360 degrees on profile. These horns can weigh up to 40 pounds on a mature ram and are used in violent battles between rams during late fall as part of their elaborate courtship. Females (ewes) also grow horns, though considerably shorter than the rams. Bighorns spend summers at higher elevations, but are almost always found on or near cliffs regardless of the season. Their agility on steep terrain is their greatest defense against predators. Whiskey Basin near Dubois, Wyoming, is home to the largest herd of bighorn sheep in the lower 48 states.

- shoulder height: 30 to 42 inches
- weight: 150 to 275 pounds

- shoulder height: 70 to 80 inches
- weight: 800 to 2,000 pounds

Bison
Bison bison

A symbol of the American West, bison are the largest land mammal in North America. Bison can be seen year-round in both Yellowstone and Grand Teton National Parks, spending the majority of their time grazing. Their mating season, or rut, takes place in August and is a wonderful opportunity to observe the bull's courtship of females (cows) and dominance displays toward one another. Bison populations across North America are estimated to have been 30 to 50 million until the late 1800s when their numbers were reduced to just a few hundred. Yellowstone provided a safe refuge for bison, and today the park hosts several thousand individuals. Jackson Hole is home to a separate herd of bison that originated from a private ranch near the town of Moran, Wyoming. The Jackson Hole herd is still very much wild. Bison generally appear docile, but can be aggressive and can run over 35 miles per hour. Following a nine-month gestation, calves are born in May and are dark red for their first two to three months. A common question about this enormous mammal is whether it is called a bison or a buffalo. Though widely called buffalo, our North American bison are more closely related to domestic cows than they are to true buffalo of Asia and Africa. The scientific name makes the answer clear.

Antilocapridae Family

♂ ♀

- shoulder height: 36 to 42 inches
- weight: 75 to 150 pounds

Pronghorn
Antilocapra americana

There is no other animal in the world like the pronghorn. They are unique to western North America and are the fastest mammal in the Western Hemisphere. They possess many unique adaptations that give them this speed, including an enlarged heart, an above-average number of red blood cells, large windpipe, and lightweight skeleton. Their excellent eyesight allows them to search for predators from miles away, which is especially useful for diurnal life on the open plains. Pronghorn fawns are vulnerable to predators such as coyotes, but are born virtually scentless in late May to early June. Yellowstone's Lamar Valley and the open sage flats of Jackson Hole are both great places to observe pronghorn.

Pronghorn are not well adapted to deep snow. The Jackson Hole herd, frequently seen from June through October, commits annually to the second-longest terrestrial mammal migration in North America. Before winter snows blanket the ground, the herd travels south more than 100 miles through the Gros Ventre Mountains to the lower elevations of the Green River Basin.

Pronghorn are frequently called antelope, but considering that they share only distant genetic similarities with their African cousins, this title is misleading. Pronghorn have true horns (made of keratin), but are unique in that the horn's sheath is shed annually. Wyoming is the epicenter of the world's population of pronghorn, with more individuals found in this state than anywhere else.

Deer (Cervidae) Family

Mule Deer
Odocoileus hemionus

In the GYE, mule deer are more common than the smaller white-tailed deer. "Mulies" have much larger ears, a smaller tail, and antlers with two main beams. The tail of mule deer is black-tipped and shorter than white-tailed deer. Another distinction between the two species is that mule deer tend to bound rather than run, landing on all four hooves at once. Mule deer frequent moderately steep slopes during winter, feeding on low-lying shrubs such as bitterbrush.

- shoulder height: 36 to 42 inches
- weight: 150 to 400 pounds

White-tailed Deer
Odocoileus virginianus

Although common in midwest and eastern states, whitetails are one of the least common ungulates in the GYE. They share many physical similarities with mule deer, so distinction may require careful observation. White-tailed deer prefer river bottoms more than mule deer and will raise their tails, revealing the white fur underneath when alarmed. Breeding between mule deer and white-tailed deer does occur but is infrequent. Tracks and scat of the two species are virtually identical.

- shoulder height: 36 to 42 inches
- weight: 100 to 300 pounds

Rocky Mountain Elk
Cervus elaphus nelsoni

Local Indians knew this abundant mammal as "wapiti," which translates to "white rump." The GYE hosts over 30,000 elk, with 6,000 to 8,000 residing on the National Elk Refuge in Jackson Hole during winter. They remain in smaller herds during summer and tend to move to higher elevations. As fall approaches, the largest bulls court multiple females (cows) and expend their energy reserves mating and defending their harems against other bulls. During this period, bulls vocalize frequently with a high-pitched bugle.

- shoulder height: 54 to 60 inches
- weight: 500 to 900 pounds

Shiras Moose
Alces alces

The largest deer species in the world, moose are a charismatic large mammal that frequent riparian habitats near rivers, creeks, ponds, and lakes. Four subspecies of moose are found in North America. Our Rocky Mountain subspecies is known as "Shiras" and is smaller than other American moose. Equipped with long legs and thick fur, moose are well adapted for deep snow and cold temperatures. Females with calves can be very defensive and should never be approached. Bull moose shed their antlers earlier than any other local deer species (often in late December or early January).

- shoulder height: 78 to 90 inches
- weight: 700 to 1,300 pounds

Raccoon (Procyonidae) Family

Raccoon
Procyon lotor

Sporting a black mask and tail with 5 to 7 rings, raccoons are unmistakable. These omnivores are dormant for several months during winter. Numbers are increasing in the GYE, but sightings are still uncommon.

- length: 34 to 55 inches
- weight: 8 to 20 pounds

Weasel (Mustelidae) Family

Long-tailed Weasel
Mustela frenata

Despite their small size, this weasel is one of the most aggressive carnivores found in the region. Their long, thin bodies and razor-sharp teeth are ideally suited for capturing and consuming small rodents. Their fur turns completely white during winter except for a small black tip on the tail. The closely related short-tailed weasel (also known as an ermine) is very similar in appearance, but its tail is shorter and the black tip is proportionally shorter as well.

short-tailed weasel (ermine) for comparison

Summer

Winter

- length with tail: 11 to 18 inches
- weight: 5 to 11 ounces

Mink
Mustela vison

Mink are generally darker and larger than the weasels described above. They prey on aquatic animals such as fish, frogs, and the occasional muskrat, but are rarely seen due to their nocturnal habits. Their fur is renowned for both its texture and insulative qualities.

- length with tail: 26 to 36 inches
- weight: 2 to 3 pounds

Badger
Taxidea taxus

Badgers are equipped with stocky, powerful bodies and sharp claws for digging. The ability to quickly dig their own holes or expand existing smaller tunnels allows them to effectively pursue subterranean rodents such as ground squirrels. Badgers are generally nocturnal and secretive, so it is more common to see their tracks and signs than it is to see the actual animal. Badger holes are wider than they are tall due to their body shape. They are primarily predators, but will occasionally scavenge carcasses. With their notoriously aggressive demeanor, badgers may intimidate larger mammals from a kill. The combination of facial markings, size, and habitat (often open sagebrush areas) make them unlikely to be mistaken for any other animal.

- length with tail: 22 to 34 inches
- weight: 15 to 25 pounds

Wolverine
Gulo gulo

Wolverines are the largest member of the weasel family in North America and are considered by many wildlife enthusiasts to be the "holy grail" of wildlife sightings. They are present in this ecosystem, but are one of the rarest animals to observe in the wild. Their long claws, distinct blonde stripes along their sides, and loping gait all contribute to accurate identification.Historically, wolverines were prized by trappers, leading to their virtual elimination from most of their original range. Wolverines are very opportunistic and will scavenge as readily as they will kill prey, ranging from small rodents to large ungulates. Like many other weasels, wolverines undergo delayed implantation, which means that although mating takes place in spring or summer, the embryo doesn't begin growing until winter.

- length with tail: 40 to 51 inches
- weight: 30 to 60 pounds

Pine Marten
Martes americana

Also called American or Pacific marten (and also classified as *Martes caurina*), these residents of coniferous forests are mid-sized weasels not frequently seen in the wild. They are excellent tree climbers and, like many species in this family, solitary. Prey is primarily red squirrels and other small rodents such as voles. Their dark fur, pale bib, and habitat preference contribute to accurate identification. Presence is often revealed by unique track patterns in snow (see winter track section).

- length with tail: 16 to 24 inches
- weight: 1 to 3 pounds

River Otter
Lutra canadensis

Otters appear to be joyous animals that are both playful and social. River otters are active year-round, diving after fish and other aquatic animals along stretches of creeks, rivers, and lakes. Their distinct muscular tail and webbed feet allow for powerful swimming, and long vibrissae (whiskers) assist in pursuing prey in murky waters. During winter, an otter's thick fur provides excellent insulation. They are occasionally seen belly sliding down snowy slopes or across frozen water.

- length with tail: 36 to 52 inches
- weight: 10 to 30 pounds

Skunk (Mephitidae) Family

Striped Skunk
Mephitis mephitis

Skunks aren't common in the GYE. Visitors are more likely to detect one by its odor than to actually see one. Their distinct black and white markings serve to warn potential predators that pursuit is unwise. When bothered, skunks will raise their tail and spray from their anal scent gland. During colder months skunks become dormant, but this is not a true hibernation. Diet is comprised of fruit, insects, and small mammals.

- length: 30 to 45 inches
- weight: 4 to 8 pounds

Canine (Canidae) Family

Red Fox
Vulpes vulpes

silver phase

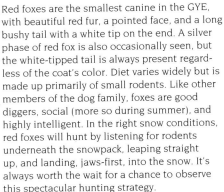

Red foxes are the smallest canine in the GYE, with beautiful red fur, a pointed face, and a long bushy tail with a white tip on the end. A silver phase of red fox is also occasionally seen, but the white-tipped tail is always present regardless of the coat's color. Diet varies widely but is made up primarily of small rodents. Like other members of the dog family, foxes are good diggers, social (more so during summer), and highly intelligent. In the right snow conditions, red foxes will hunt by listening for rodents underneath the snowpack, leaping straight up, and landing, jaws-first, into the snow. It's always worth the wait for a chance to observe this spectacular hunting strategy.

- shoulder height: 15 inches
- weight: 8 to 16 pounds

Coyote
Canis latrans

The scientific name for coyote translates to "singing" or "talking dog." This is an appropriate title as they are extremely vocal and are capable of many different sounds including yips, growls, barks, and howls. Coyotes are gray with hints of red in their fur, especially behind their ears, and have pointed noses. They pose virtually no direct threat to people and serve as an important control to rodent populations. Nevertheless, coyotes can be a menace to ranch livestock and have been found to kill more sheep and cows than any other predator. Coyotes are solitary in some regions, but within the GYE are typically part of a pack with a social dynamic similar to wolves. From the 1930s through the 1990s when wolves were absent, coyotes became the "top dog" in the ecosystem. Their numbers have reduced substantially since the return of the gray wolf.

- shoulder height: 24 inches
- weight: 20 to 35 pounds

- shoulder height: 24 to 36 inches
- weight: 70 to 120 pounds

Gray Wolf
Canis lupus

Identification of a gray wolf can sometimes be unmistakable or occasionally more challenging. Wolves are as much as three times larger than coyotes, have a broader muzzle, and, proportionally, longer legs. Fur color can be helpful since a large percentage of the region's wolves are black, while there are no black coyotes. Many wolves are gray and there are a few white wolves. In 1995 and 1996, gray wolves were trapped in Alberta and British Columbia and reintroduced into northern Yellowstone. This marked their return after a 60-year absence, one of the most publicized and controversial issues in the West. Ecologically, the reintroduction has been an enormous success, restoring a natural balance that was lost in their absence. Their tendency to roam beyond park boundaries, however, has led to strong anti-wolf sentiments, as they will occasionally kill livestock and pets. Their favorite prey are elk and bison, and consequently they have been blamed for more challenging hunting conditions outside the park. Since the mid-1990s, Yellowstone's Lamar Valley has been one of the best places in the world for viewing wild wolves, but now they may be seen throughout the Rocky Mountains. Wolves are intensely territorial and will defend their areas against other packs, killing rivals. Regardless of political sentiments, seeing or hearing a wolf is one of the most genuinely wild moments we can experience on this continent.

Distinguishing Wolves from Coyotes

Distinguishing coyotes from wolves isn't always easy, especially from a long distance. Within the GYE, wolves and coyotes roam similar habitats, and both species may be seen (and heard) in packs or traveling alone, day or night. Both are also commonly seen on or near carcasses. A wolf pack can take down large game such as deer, elk, moose, and occasionally young or even adult bison. Coyotes favor mice, voles, rabbits, and ground squirrels, but will also eat birds, eggs, frogs, insects, and berries. While a wolf pack may bed down in the open after a heavy meal, coyotes tend to select heavier cover when resting. In general, wolves are taller and bulkier, with a blockier head. Coyotes are of a lighter build with a narrower face. Generalities, however, may not suffice for identifying individual animals in the wild. As with most wildlife, observing several different characteristics will lead to more accurate identification.

Coyote

- usually less than 35 pounds
- pointed muzzle and ears
- fur is consistently gray overall, except red tinge behind ears
- tends to walk with tail dropped
- vocalizations vary but usually higher pitched than wolves

Gray Wolf

- taller and about three times heavier (70 to 120 pounds) than coyotes
- broad muzzle with more rounded ears
- fur coloration varies widely; can be black, gray, or white
- often walks with tail held horizontally
- legs are proportionally longer than in coyotes

Distinguishing Black Bears from Grizzly Bears

Despite their common name, black bears come in a range of fur colors, from blond, cinnamon, brown, or black. Grizzly bear coloration also varies and can be silvery, gold, dark brown, or almost black. In the GYE, these two species also overlap in size, especially when accounting for the range in sizes at various ages and between females and males. Both black and grizzly bears roam throughout the GYE, and both species are opportunistic in their feeding habits, grazing on plants, digging for rodents, overturning rocks and logs for insects, and feasting on carcasses. In short, color and size are not the best characteristics to rely on when trying to identify a bear in the GYE, nor are habitat and diet conclusive. Look instead for the following details to determine the species of bear.

Black Bear

- profile lacks shoulder hump
- fur color can be black, brown, or blond
- ears often appear proportionally longer than grizzly bears
- muzzle is often light-brown
- shorter claws than grizzly bears

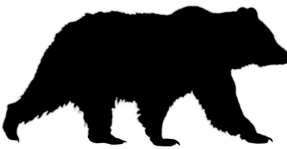

Grizzly Bear

- profile reveals shoulder hump and more concave face
- ears appear shorter and more rounded
- claws are about twice the length of black bears (up to 4 inches on front paws)
- more likely to stand upright on back legs than black bears

Bear (Ursidae) Family

Black Bear
Ursus americanus

Black bears den up between October and March, and females actually give birth to cubs in their winter dens. As omnivores, their diet includes insects, carrion, small mammals, plants, and berries. Remarkable memories allow them to navigate large territories, returning to far-flung places that previously yielded food. Early visitors to Yellowstone regularly fed begging black bears from their vehicles. This is now strictly prohibited and, fortunately, very uncommon. Bears that become habituated to people often need to be removed by lethal force.

- shoulder height: 30 to 44 inches
- weight: 150 to 500 lbs

(front track)

Grizzly Bear
Ursus arctos

Grizzlies within the Greater Yellowstone Ecosystem are only slightly bigger than our black bears and may overlap in habitat. Grizzly bears avoid encounters with people by using their extraordinary sense of smell. They sometimes stand on their hind legs to better view their surroundings. Grizzly bears vary in color from pale tan to golden to black. Field marks to watch for are a muscular shoulder hump, dished face, and long claws. Their opportunistic diet means that they will eat almost anything, so they are widespread. Hayden Valley, Lamar Valley, and northern Grand Teton National Park are great places to find grizzlies. Direct encounters with people are rare but still worthy of consideration when hiking in bear country. Conflicts are more likely to occur near a carcass, if a female has cubs, or when people hike alone. Travel in groups, make noise, and carry bear pepper spray when hiking in the GYE.

(front track)

- shoulder height: 36 to 48 inches
- weight: 300 to 700 lbs

Cat (Felidae) Family

Bobcat
Lynx rufus

Bobcats and lynx are both very rare cats and are similar enough in size and body shape that detailed observations are essential for accurate identification. Both species have ear tufts and short tails, but the tufts are longer on lynx, and a bobcat's tail is black-tipped only on top. (The tip of a lynx's tail is black all around.) Bobcats tend to be more spotted, particularly along the belly.

- length with tail: 28 to 34 inches
- weight: 15 to 35 pounds

Canada Lynx
Lynx canadensis

Sightings of lynx are extremely rare. They prey on a variety of small mammals, but snowshoe hares are a large part of their diet. Their feet are extremely large (tracks may register as large as a mountain lion) and have thick fur in and around their toes. This creates track impressions with softer edges. As with other North American cats, claws retract and don't register in tracks.

- length with tail: 36 to 48 inches
- weight: 20 to 30 lbs

Mountain Lion
Puma concolor

Mountain lions are the largest cat in the GYE. Other common names include cougar, catamount, puma, and panther. Their large size, dark mustache, and long tail are all good field marks, but their elusive nature and large home ranges render sightings uncommon. Mule deer are a favorite prey. Lions mainly hunt by ambush rather than pursuing prey over distances. Mountain lion attacks on people are very rare. They are secretive and will usually leave an area before being seen.

- length with tail: 60 to 80 inches
- weight: 100 to 250 pounds

Tracks and Scat

The ability to identify an animal from its tracks, scat, and other signs is a useful skill to any outdoor enthusiast since these indicate an animal's presence long after it has disappeared. Signs vary considerably based on substrate, snow depth, snow type, and, for scat, the animal's recent diet. This section is broken into three parts: individual tracks (those left in mud, sand, or other soft substrate, which allows for observation of more detailed characteristics such as number of toes, presence of claws, and more precise measurements), winter tracks (patterns left in the snow), and scat.

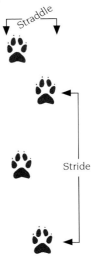

The two terms described in the image to the right are very helpful for all tracking and are one of the primary reasons that a small tape measure is worth carrying in your pack.

If an individual track can be seen clearly, one of the easiest and most important observations to make is simply counting how many toes register in the track. The following pages are organized according to how many toes typically show in the animal's track.

Mammal Tracks at a Glance
Tracks that Register Five Toes

Badger

- stride: 15 to 20 inches
- straddle: 8 inches
- a badger's stocky build creates a wide straddle and leaves a pigeon-toed gait
- badgers have long claws for digging; tracks are often found near oval-shaped burrows

2"

Pine Marten

- stride: 20 to 25 inches
- straddle: 4 inches
- martens have five toes but occasionally only four toes register
- almost always found in conifer forests

1.5 to 2"

Striped Skunk

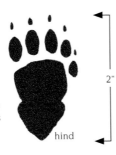

- straddle: 3 to 4 inches
- front track is similar to hind but shorter (about 1 inch long)
- long claws allow for digging burrows
- feet have long hairs in between pads, so details can be obscured

2"

hind

Wolverine

- stride: 15 to 30 inches
- straddle: 7 to 8 inches
- one of the rarest tracks to encounter (more likely in alpine areas)
- similar to other weasels but much larger

3 to 5"

Black Bear

- stride: 30 to 35 inches
- straddle: 15 inches
- all five toes usually register in tracks; very similar to grizzly bear tracks except smaller and line cannot be drawn between interdigital pad and toes without bisecting toe
- big toe is on outside of foot (opposite of humans)
- claws usually seen in track but closer to toes than grizzly bears

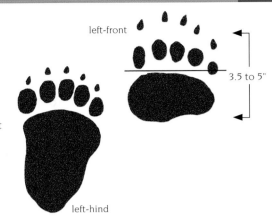

left-front

left-hind

3.5 to 5"

Grizzly Bear

- stride: 40 to 45 inches
- straddle: 21 inches
- a straight line can generally be drawn between inter-digital pad and toes without touching either
- longer claws than black bears
- gait is usually slow and slightly pigeon-toed
- hind track may appear ahead of or within front track

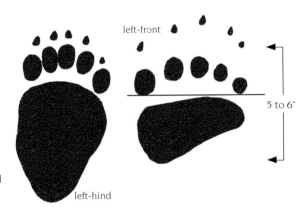

left-front

left-hind

5 to 6"

Raccoon

- straddle: 9 inches
- long toes with claws often visible
- raccoon's digits are dextrous; tracks resemble small human handprints
- not a commonly seen track, but mudflats along rivers are a good place to encounter them

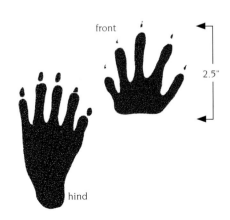

front

hind

2.5"

Tracks that Register Four or Five Toes

Beaver

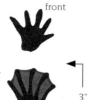

front

- straddle: 6 to 8 inches
- tracks typically found in silt and may be wiped away by flat tail
- hind foot is much larger and webbed

3"

hind

Chipmunk

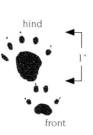

hind

1"

front

- hind feet register five toes, while the front register four, which can be confusing since chipmunks, like many rodents, "over-stride" and place hind feet ahead of front feet

Muskrat

front

hind

2.5"

- tracks similar to those of beaver in that both front and hind appear hand-like
- inner toe of the front track is disproportion-ally small

Pika

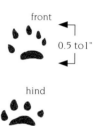

front

0.5 to 1"

hind

- unlike rodents, pikas may register five toes from front feet and four toes from rear feet rather than the other way around
- finding pika tracks is challenging due to their fondness for rocky terrain

Yellow-bellied Marmot

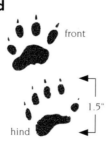

front

1.5"

hind

- like most rodents, hind tracks register five toes and front tracks register four
- found in rocky habitats; tracks infrequently encountered

Red Squirrel

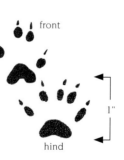

front

1"

hind

- similar to chip-munk tracks but often slightly larger
- tracks potentially seen year-round since red squirrels don't hibernate (unlike chipmunks)

Porcupine

2.5 to 3.5"

- straddle: 7 to 9 inches
- porcupines have five toes, but it is common for only four toes to register clearly
- usually a pigeon-toed gait
- the quill-laden tail dragging behind often wipes tracks away
- tracks often occur between trees where porcupines will roost for long periods

Tracks that Register Four Toes

Tracks from members of the canine family share several characteristics including registering four toes, claws showing in tracks, more oval lengthwise than feline tracks, and front feet larger than rear feet. Distinguishing tracks of wild canines from domestic dogs can be difficult but, generally, the toes of domestic dogs splay more outward.

Red Fox

- stride: 12 to 16 inches
- straddle: 4 to 5 inches
- overall more delicate than other canine tracks with an interdigital pad more "chevron" in shape
- red fox tracks often have more space between interdigital pad and toes than other canines

2 to 2.5"

Coyote

- stride: 15 to 20 inches
- straddle: 5 to 6 inches
- size falls between wolf and fox tracks
- two outer toes often appear larger than inner toes, and claws of outer toes may not register as clearly
- all toes generally parallel to one another along length-wise axis

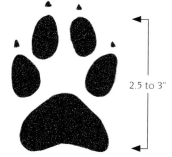

2.5 to 3"

Gray Wolf

- stride: 25 to 35 inches
- straddle: 7 to 8 inches
- much larger than any other wild canine track
- the four toes tend to be more similarly sized than coyotes and are more likely to register all four claws
- most wolves are part of a pack and often travel in a single line, which will create more of a track highway than other canines

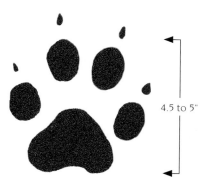

4.5 to 5"

Tracks that Register Four Toes (continued)

General characteristics of feline tracks are that their claws retract and consequently don't register, an overall wider appearance than canine tracks, and interdigital pads with two lobes at the top and three lobes at the bottom.

Bobcat

- stride: 15 to 18 inches
- straddle: 5 inches
- can be similar to domestic cats but usually larger and rounder
- much smaller than lynx and mountain lion tracks

2"

Canada Lynx

- stride: 18 to 25 inches
- straddle: 6 to 7 inches
- lynx tracks are about the same size as mountain lions due to their over-sized feet, but the stride and straddle are less due to smaller body size
- lynx feet have extensive hair between pads and this often obscures most details within tracks

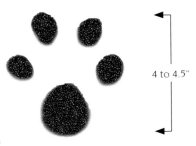

4 to 4.5"

Mountain Lion

- stride: 20 to 30 inches
- straddle: 7 to 9 inches
- tracks usually show greater detail than lynx and tend to sink deeper into snow and mud than the much lighter lynx
- mountain lions are good tree climbers; tracks may terminate at the base of a tree

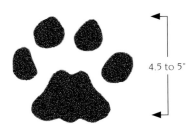

4.5 to 5"

Snowshoe Hare

- stride measurements vary enormously
- enormous hind feet and relatively small front feet
- hares are over-striders, so the hind feet will always register ahead of the front feet
- snowshoe hare tracks are seen much more than the animals themselves due to their nocturnal tendencies

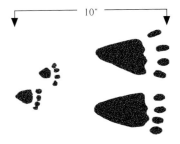

10"

Tracks that Register Two Toes

Bighorn Sheep

- stride: 30 to 35 inches
- straddle: 6 to 7 inches
- bighorn sheep's preference for rocky terrain means that clear tracks are not commonly seen

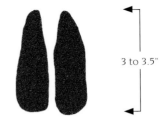

3 to 3.5"

Bison

- stride: 50 to 60 inches
- straddle: 14 to 20 inches
- larger than any other hoofed mammal and more "jelly bean" in shape
- tracks and scat are both similar to domestic cattle
- other bison signs include rubbings on trees (commonly seen in Yellowstone) and wallows (depressions in the ground that bison roll in)

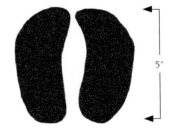

5"

Mountain Goat

- stride: 28 to 32 inches
- straddle: 7 inches
- like bighorn sheep, mountain goats frequent cliff areas and tracks don't often register clearly
- toes are slightly more pointed than other hoofed mammals

2.5 to 3"

Pronghorn

- stride: 28 to 32 inches
- straddle: 6 to 8 inches
- similar to bighorn sheep but with more narrow tips (habitats don't overlap frequently)

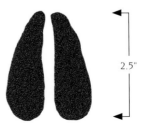

2.5"

Tracks that Register Two Toes (continued)

Mule Deer

- stride: 35 to 40 inches
- straddle: 6 inches
- tracks slightly larger than white-tailed deer but otherwise indistinguishable
- tracks tend to be found on steeper terrain compared to whitetails

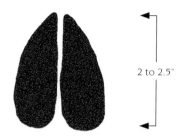

2 to 2.5"

Rocky Mountain Elk

- stride: 40 to 50 inches
- straddle: 8 to 9 inches
- tracks longer and wider than mule deer tracks
- bulls leave slightly larger tracks than cows, but due to social nature of elk, tracks may be obscured due to linear migrations of elk between high and low elevations (often with cow elk leading)

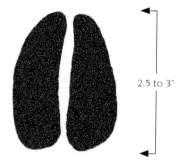

2.5 to 3"

Moose

- stride: 45 to 55 inches
- straddle: 9 to 11 inches
- tracks are slightly more pointed than elk and considerably larger in adults
- dewclaws may register more clearly in moose tracks than other deer species
- moose are typically found in more riparian habitats than other ungulates and able to navigate deeper snow depths than most large mammals

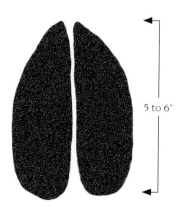

5 to 6"

Winter Track Patterns

Stories left behind in the snow can provide fascinating insight into the presence and behaviors of animals during winter. Tracking in winter requires observations of the overall pattern left behind by the animal, not simply the dimensions for individual prints. Fortunately these patterns, in conjunction with the stride and straddle measurements, are fairly unique to each species.

Raven

- the wings of several birds leave beautiful, angelic impressions when landing on or taking off from the snow's surface.
- several other species commonly leave this type of sign including owls, jays, grouse, and magpies
- the wingspan of a raven is about 53 inches

River Otter

- river otters are commonly found near frozen ponds, lakes, or rivers
- otters frequently incorporate a long playful slide on their belly into their bounding style of locomotion

4"

Red Squirrel

- tracks seen all winter
- hind feet are bigger than front feet
- red squirrels are over-striders; their hind feet register in front of their front feet

1"

Deer Mouse

- small rodents can be difficult to distinguish, but deer mouse tracks are common in winter as this species does not hibernate
- tail drag often visible

Long-tailed Weasel

- a narrow "dumbbell" pattern will register in deeper snow, occasionally disappearing as the weasel explores the subnivean (under-snow) environment
- a delicate 2x2 pattern often registers in shallow snow (far right set of tracks)

Snowshoe Hare

- enormous hind feet keep hares from sinking into snow
- over-striders (see red squirrel above)
- distance between track sets varies considerably

Pine Marten

- exhibit classic 2x2 weasel pattern with very few exceptions
- if an individual track is clearly registered, five toes can be seen
- distance between sets varies considerably

Porcupine

- pattern tends to indicate the waddling style of locomotion
- tracks are pigeon-toed
- marks from dragging quills often visible

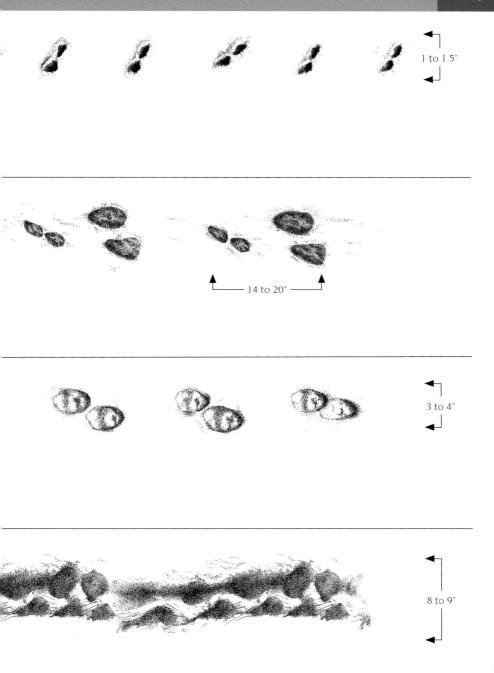

1 to 1.5"

14 to 20"

3 to 4"

8 to 9"

Red Fox

- four toes register, usually with claws
- interdigital (center) pad is more chevron shaped than other canines

Coyote

- pattern can be C-shaped (first four tracks) or alternating (final five tracks)
- patterns tend to be less wandering than domestic dogs

Gray Wolf

- largest of canines
- like coyotes, pattern can be C-shaped or alternating
- general track shape is more oval lengthwise than cat species

Bobcat

- individual track is as wide as it is long
- back end of interdigital (center) pad is three lobed
- claws rarely register

Mountain Lion

- same qualities as bobcat above but, since mountain lions are better climbers, are more likely to lead up a tree

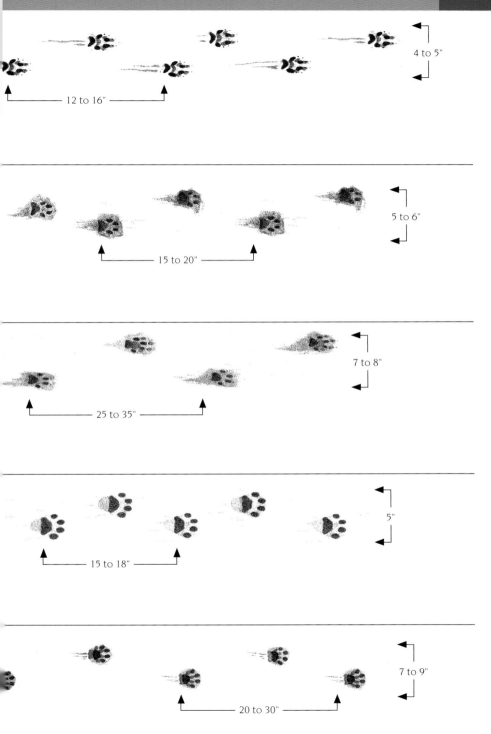

4 to 5"

12 to 16"

5 to 6"

15 to 20"

7 to 8"

25 to 35"

5"

15 to 18"

7 to 9"

20 to 30"

Mule Deer

- two toes often leave drag mark between tracks
- dimensions are similar to pronghorn, but generally are found in different habitat

Rocky Mountain Elk

- very similar to deer and moose tracks but, if individual track is visible, the tips of print will be more rounded

Moose

- hooves are more pointed than elk and deer
- often found in areas with deep snow, so individual tracks are "dumbbell" shaped

Bison

- largest of the two-toed tracks
- bison frequently travel in herds, which can make individual tracks difficult to discern
- in shallow snow, tracks appear more jelly-bean shaped than other animals

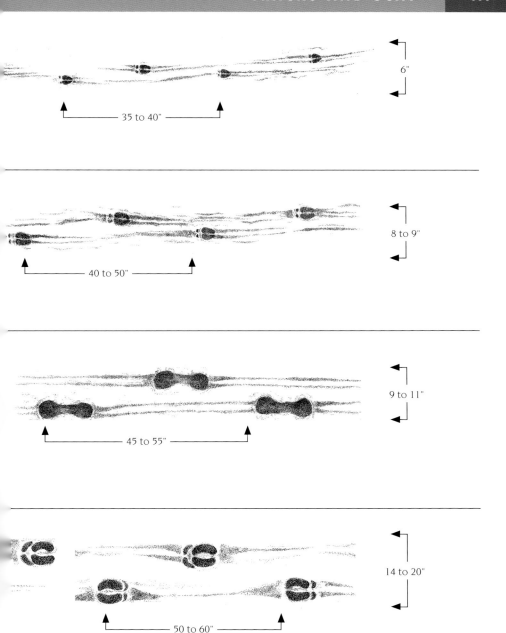

6"

35 to 40"

8 to 9"

40 to 50"

9 to 11"

45 to 55"

14 to 20"

50 to 60"

Mammal Scat at a Glance

Like tracks, wildlife scat tells us a lot about an animal's presence, diet, and general habits. Scat from herbivores consists entirely of digested plant material and is generally sterile to touch, while carnivore scat tends to have more bacteria. Scat varies considerably, but the images below are typical for each species.

Black Bear

- 3 to 5 inches long, 1 to 1.5 inches diameter
- scat contents vary
- usually smaller than grizzly bear scat, but sizes overlap

Grizzly Bear

- 4 to 6 inches long, 2 to 2.5 inches diameter
- grizzly bear's diet includes both plants and animals so scat contents vary

Coyote

- 3 to 4 inches long, 0.5 inch diameter
- often contains hair and bones but may include grass and berries
- one end usually long and tapered

Gray Wolf

- 5 to 6 inches long, 0.75 inch diameter
- usually more hair and bones than coyote scat
- tapered on one end

Lynx

- 3 to 4 inches long, 0.75 inch diameter
- can be similar to both bobcat and coyote scat
- lynx and bobcats frequently bury scat

Mountain Lion

- 4 to 8 inches long, 1.25 inches diameter
- often braided and containing hair
- tapered end is often shorter than canine scat

River Otter

- 1 to 1.5 inches long, 1 to 1.5 inches diameter
- dark and almost always containing bones and fish scales

Long-tailed Weasel

- 0.25 inch diameter
- weasel scat is often darkly colored, containing hair and bone fragments
- often tapered at both ends

Beaver

- 0.5 to 0.75 inch long, 0.75 inch diameter
- scat made up entirely of plant material
- usually left in water and often disintegrates

Bison

- 8 to 12 inches diameter
- distinct soft "patties" are unlike other ungulate scat except cattle
- flammable when dry

Moose

- 1 to 1.25 inches long
- largest of all pellet scat
- more rounded ends than elk and deer scat
- comprised completely of vegetation (usually more woody material than elk and deer)

Elk

- 0.75 inch long
- pellets usually are pointed on one end and have an indentation on the other end

Mule Deer

- 0.5 to 0.75 inch long
- may be slightly pointed on one end, but lacking indentation seen on elk scat
- virtually identical to white-tailed deer scat

Bighorn Sheep

- 0.5 to 0.75 inch long
- like mule deer scat but may be more round overall
- very similar to mountain goat scat

Pronghorn

- 0.5 to 0.75 inch long
- scat often more pointed than other species, but can be very similar to sheep
- more likely to be found in open sagebrush habitats

Yellow-bellied Marmot

- 0.75 to 1.25 inches long
- usually dark and found in one main area near burrows

Uinta Ground Squirrel

- 0.5 to 0.75 inch long
- often braided pellets that may be connected to one another
- can be found near entrances to underground burrows

Porcupine

- 0.5 to 0.75 inch long, 0.25 inch diameter
- more elongated than other rodent scat with long tapered end that may connect

The Night Sky

On a clear, moonless night in the absence of light pollution, we can see between 5,000 to 6,000 stars with the naked eye. As one of the least populated regions in the lower 48 states, the Greater Yellowstone Ecosystem offers incredibly dark skies and a rare opportunity to experience these stars and other astronomical phenomena. Along with experiencing Yellowstone and Grand Teton's wildlife, geothermal phenomena, and flora, every visit to these national parks should include some time spent looking humbly upward to appreciate the wildness and mystery beyond our own planet.

The three most familiar celestial objects are the Sun (which provides much of the energy that drives our biosphere), the Moon, and (of course) our own planet. Earth lies about 93 million miles from the Sun, an ideal distance for temperatures conducive to life. A common misconception about this relationship is that our seasons are a result of varying distance between the Earth and the Sun. In reality they are a result of the 23.5-degree tilt of our planet's axis. During the Northern Hemisphere's winter, this part of the Earth tilts away from the Sun. We tilt toward the Sun during our summer months.

The Moon is almost as easy for us to take for granted as the Sun. It is only about one quarter the size of Earth and is locked in position with only one side facing Earth as it orbits. It just so happens that the Sun is 400 times larger than the Moon and is 400 times farther away from Earth. This is why they appear to us to be the same size. It also makes total eclipses possible.

Our planetary neighbors are always exciting to observe; Saturn, Mars, Jupiter, and Venus are especially bright. Early astronomers didn't know exactly what the planets were and called them "wandering stars," recognizing that they didn't follow the same predictable path across the night sky as other stars. This is why star charts like the ones on subsequent pages don't include planets. Digital astronomy guides and websites will provide accurate locations of the planets. The GYE lies between latitudes 42° and 45° North, which means that the path of the planets, also known as the ecliptic, is across the southern portion of the night sky.

Deciphering the 88 constellations requires some degree of imagination, as few accurately represent the objects that they are named for. Nevertheless, the stories associated with each constellation are fascinating, and to serious astronomers constellation maps serve as guides to other objects such as galaxies, nebulae, and star clusters.

Astronomy can be an expensive hobby, but may also be enjoyed with minimal equipment. A good pair of binoculars, a flashlight with a red-light setting or lens (to preserve night vision), and a star chart are enough to enable endless exploration of the night sky.

How to use the star charts:

The charts on the following pages are specific to the latitudes within the GYE but will be fairly accurate for most other mid-latitude regions in the Northern Hemisphere. Hold the chart above your head and orient the top of the chart with true North.

January

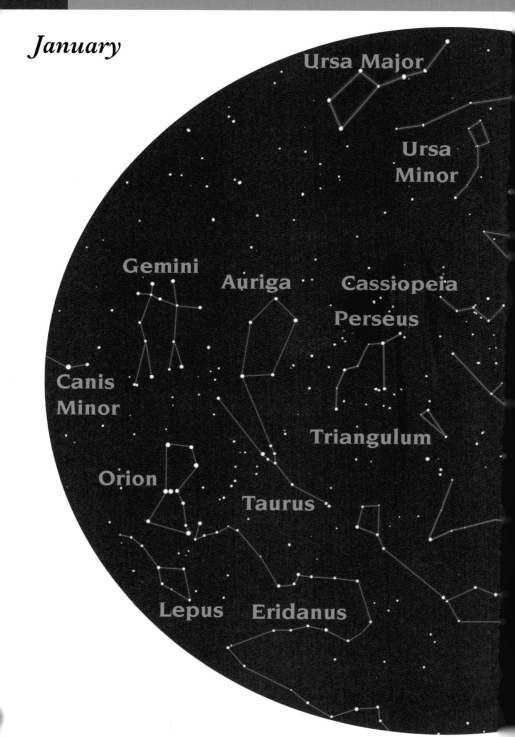

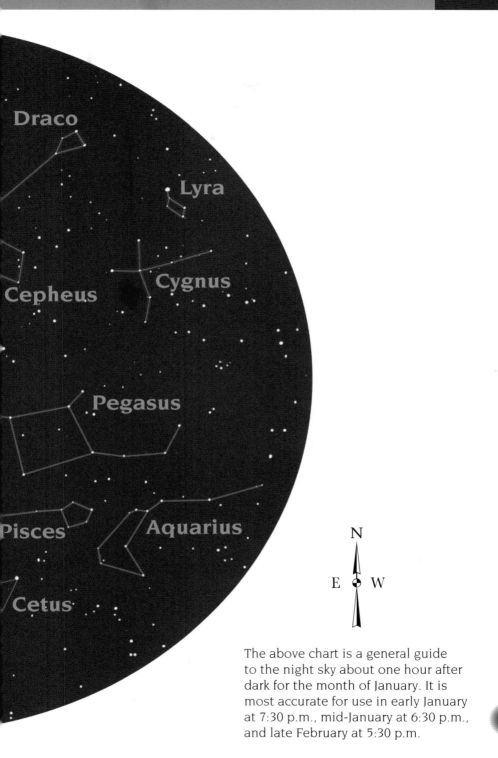

Draco

Lyra

Cygnus

Cepheus

Pegasus

Pisces

Aquarius

Cetus

N

E ⊙ W

The above chart is a general guide
to the night sky about one hour after
dark for the month of January. It is
most accurate for use in early January
at 7:30 p.m., mid-January at 6:30 p.m.,
and late February at 5:30 p.m.

February

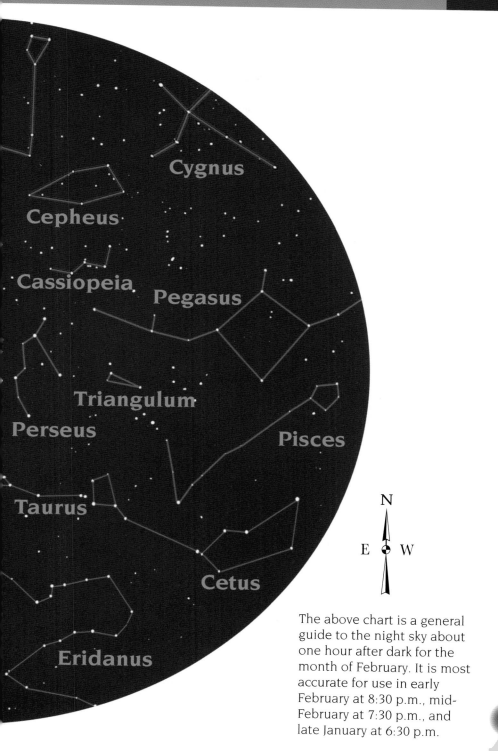

Cygnus

Cepheus

Cassiopeia

Pegasus

Triangulum

Perseus

Pisces

Taurus

Cetus

Eridanus

N

E W

The above chart is a general
guide to the night sky about
one hour after dark for the
month of February. It is most
accurate for use in early
February at 8:30 p.m., mid-
February at 7:30 p.m., and
late January at 6:30 p.m.

March

Draco

Ursa Minor

Ursa Major

Leo

Gemini

Hydra

Canis Minor

Canis Major

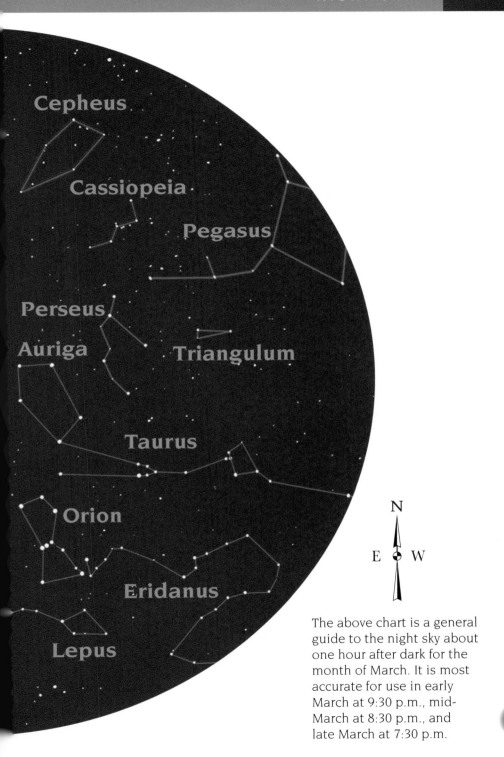

N
E ⊙ W

The above chart is a general guide to the night sky about one hour after dark for the month of March. It is most accurate for use in early March at 9:30 p.m., mid-March at 8:30 p.m., and late March at 7:30 p.m.

April

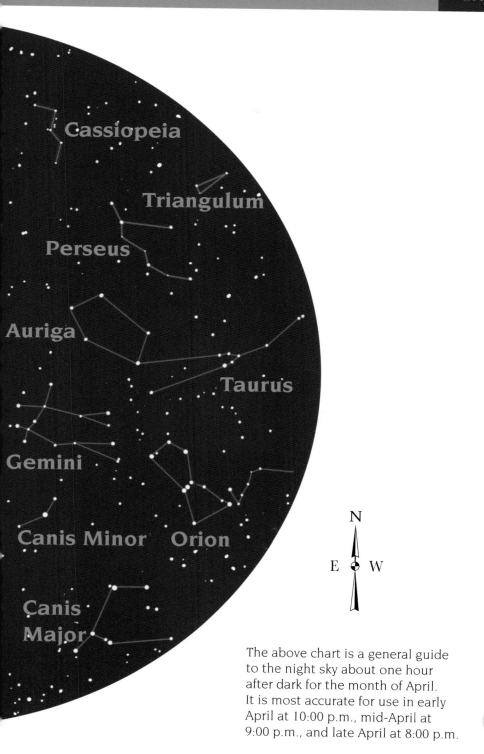

The above chart is a general guide to the night sky about one hour after dark for the month of April. It is most accurate for use in early April at 10:00 p.m., mid-April at 9:00 p.m., and late April at 8:00 p.m.

May

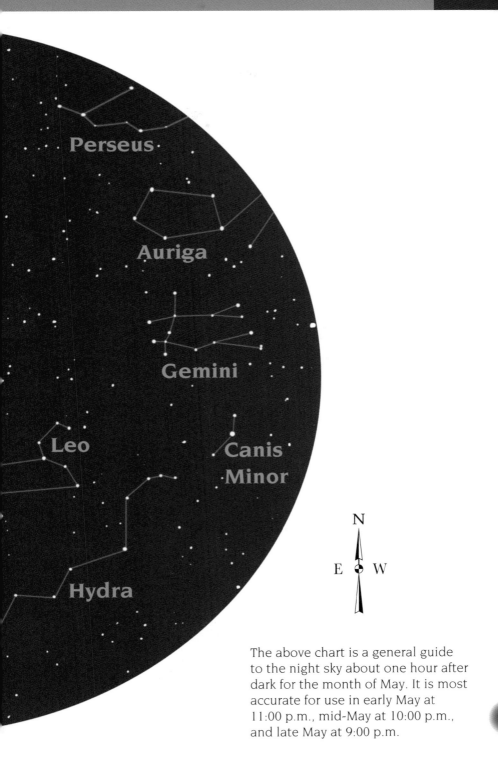

Perseus

Auriga

Gemini

Leo

Canis
Minor

Hydra

N

E ⊙ W

The above chart is a general guide
to the night sky about one hour after
dark for the month of May. It is most
accurate for use in early May at
11:00 p.m., mid-May at 10:00 p.m.,
and late May at 9:00 p.m.

June

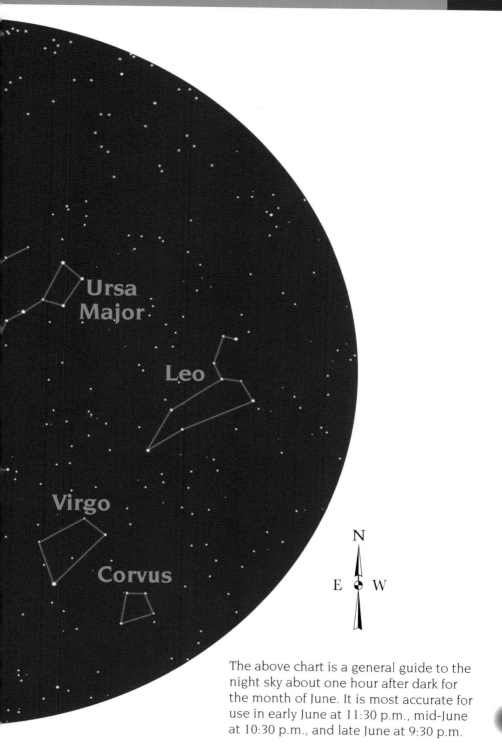

Ursa Major

Leo

Virgo

Corvus

N

E ● W

The above chart is a general guide to the night sky about one hour after dark for the month of June. It is most accurate for use in early June at 11:30 p.m., mid-June at 10:30 p.m., and late June at 9:30 p.m.

July

Cassiopeia

Cepheus

Draco

Cygnus

Lyra

Hercules

Aquila

Ophiuchus

Sagittarius

Scorpius

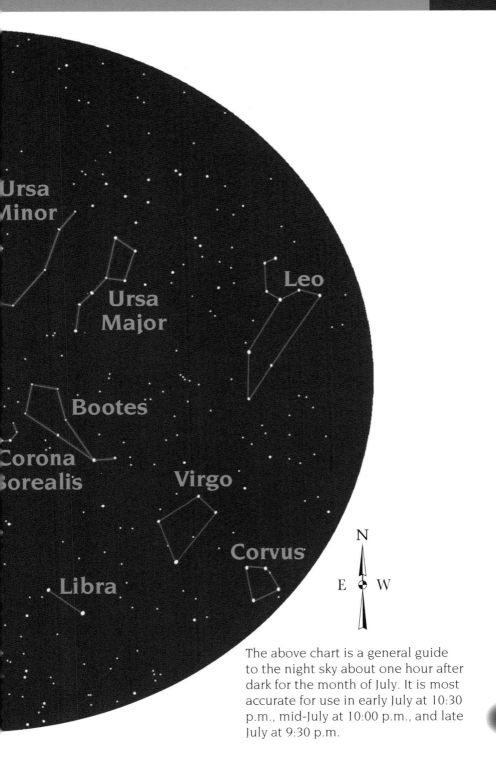

The above chart is a general guide to the night sky about one hour after dark for the month of July. It is most accurate for use in early July at 10:30 p.m., mid-July at 10:00 p.m., and late July at 9:30 p.m.

August

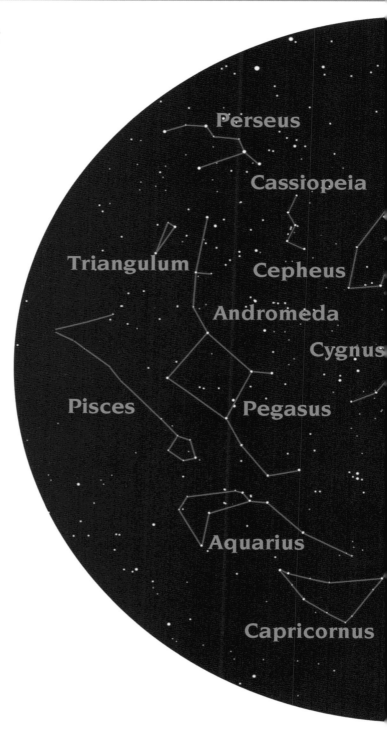

Perseus

Cassiopeia

Triangulum

Cepheus

Andromeda

Cygnus

Pisces

Pegasus

Aquarius

Capricornus

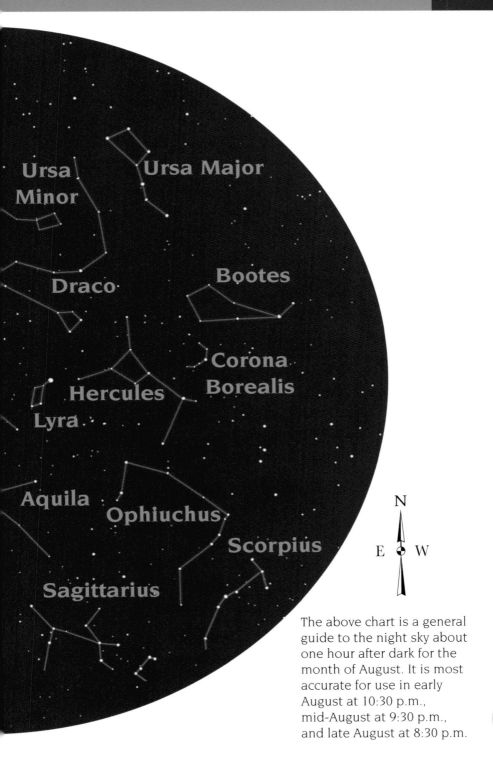

Ursa Minor

Ursa Major

Draco

Bootes

Corona Borealis

Hercules

Lyra

Aquila

Ophiuchus

Scorpius

Sagittarius

N

E   W

The above chart is a general guide to the night sky about one hour after dark for the month of August. It is most accurate for use in early August at 10:30 p.m., mid-August at 9:30 p.m., and late August at 8:30 p.m.

September

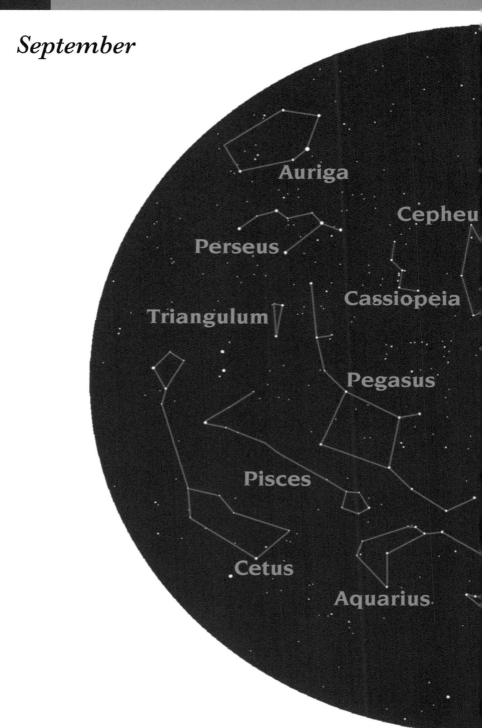

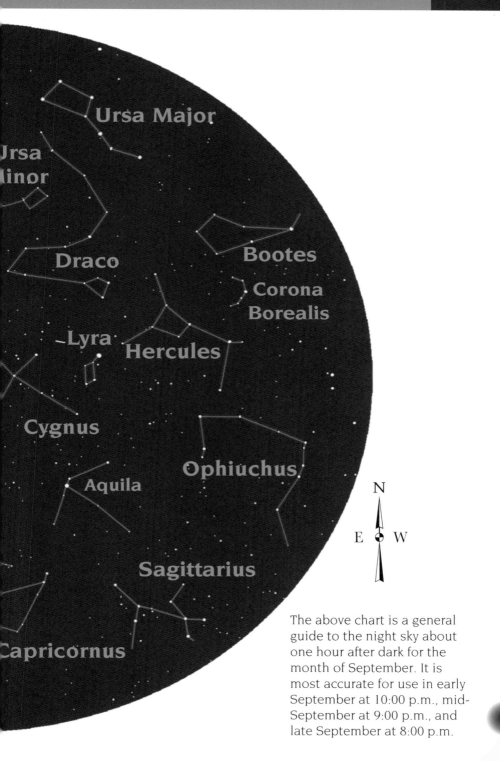

Ursa Major

Ursa Minor

Draco

Bootes

Corona Borealis

Lyra

Hercules

Cygnus

Aquila

Ophiuchus

Sagittarius

Capricornus

N

E   W

The above chart is a general guide to the night sky about one hour after dark for the month of September. It is most accurate for use in early September at 10:00 p.m., mid-September at 9:00 p.m., and late September at 8:00 p.m.

October

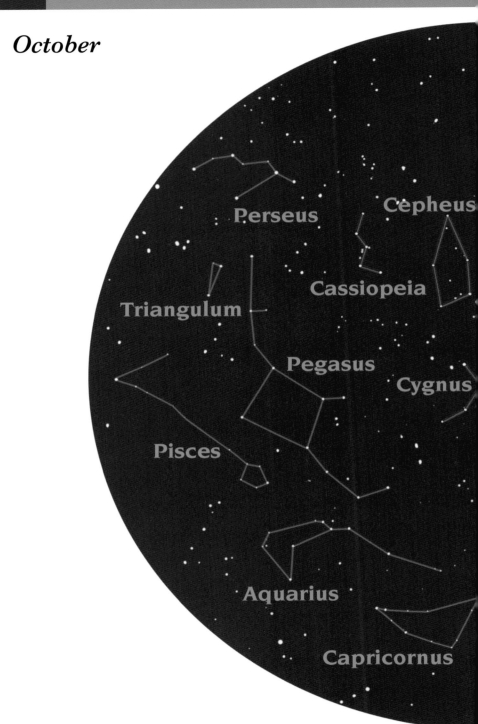

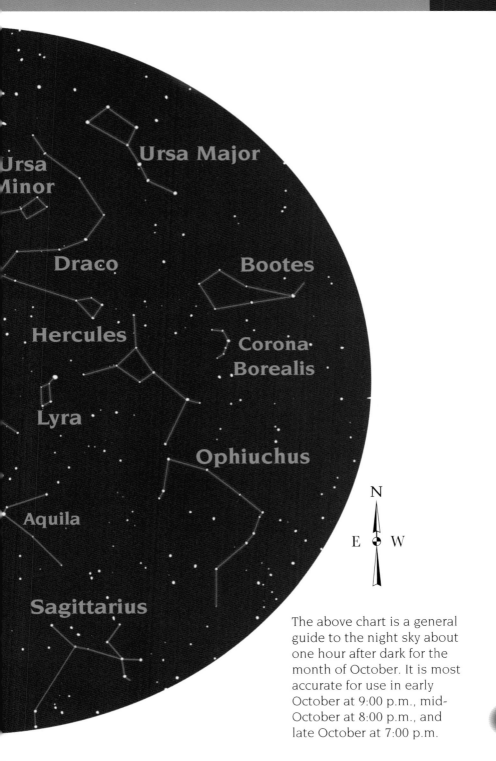

Ursa Major

Ursa Minor

Draco

Bootes

Hercules

Corona Borealis

Lyra

Ophiuchus

Aquila

Sagittarius

N

E W

The above chart is a general guide to the night sky about one hour after dark for the month of October. It is most accurate for use in early October at 9:00 p.m., mid-October at 8:00 p.m., and late October at 7:00 p.m.

November

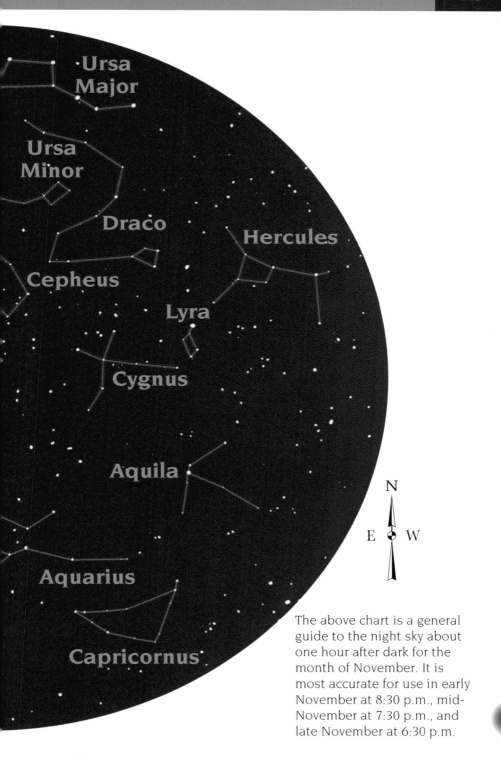

Ursa Major

Ursa Minor

Draco

Hercules

Cepheus

Lyra

Cygnus

Aquila

N

E   W

Aquarius

Capricornus

The above chart is a general guide to the night sky about one hour after dark for the month of November. It is most accurate for use in early November at 8:30 p.m., mid-November at 7:30 p.m., and late November at 6:30 p.m.

December

Ursa Major

Auriga

Cassiopeia

Perseus

Taurus

Triangulum

Pisces

Cetus

Ursa
Minor

Draco

Hercules

Cepheus

Lyra

Cygnus

Pegasus

Aquila

N

E ● W

Aquarius

Capricornus

The above chart is a general
guide to the night sky about
one hour after dark for the
month of December. It is
most accurate for use in early
December at 7:00 p.m., mid-
December at 6:00 p.m., and
late December at 5:00 p.m.

Photo Credits

A huge debt of gratitude is owed to the talented photographers who have contributed their images to this field guide. The vast majority of images within this book were taken by the author, but the following photographs were provided through individual consent or through a photography stock agency:

Florian Andronache: long-eared owl; Atli Arnason: stone centipede; Loren Ayers: masked shrew; Anders Bell: flying squirrel; Matthias Blume: Jerusalem cricket; Francis Bossé: snow bunting (breeding); Avril Bourquin: Rocky Mountain snail; Steve Brigman: pine marten; Steve Byland: belted kingfisher (female), blue-winged teal; Rick Cowen: springtail; Don Delaney: northern goshawk (immature); Rusty Dodson: common nighthawk; Dennis Donahue: short-eared owl (perched and in flight); Wayne Duguay: snow goose; Jim Edmondson: tundra swan; Ann Elliott: northern pygmy owl; Jeff Grabert: common loon; Arto Hakola: jackrabbit; RL Hambley: brown creeper; Larry Hamrin: cherry-faced meadowhawk, Pacific forktail, paddle-tailed darner, shadow darner, vivid dancer; Edmund Hertz: river jewelwing; Steve Hillebrand: short-tailed weasel; Cody Hough: thimbleberry; Frode Jacobsen: McGillivray's warbler; Ganesh K. Jayaraman: dusky flycatcher, green-tailed towhee, lazuli bunting, Lewis woodpecker, Wilson's warbler (male); Wongun Kim: snout beetle; Jerry Kirkhart: northern harrier (immature); Jacques Landry: horse mushroom, shaggy mane (pair), false morel, puffball (Lycoperdon); Matt Lavin: Booth's willow, Scouler's willow, American vetch, ballhead sandwort, hawksbeard, evening primrose, smooth brome, Kentucky bluegrass, Idaho fescue, needlegrass, prairie junegrass, reed canarygrass, slender wheatgrass, crested wheatgrass, sedge; Cletus Lee: bold jumper; Mark Leppin: northern scorpion; John Lillis: gooseberry; JC Lucier: long-jawed orbweaver; Jeremy Martin: twelve-spotted skimmer, dot-tailed whiteface, emerald spreadwing, northern bluet, spotted spreadwing; Martha Marks: gray catbird; Peter Massas: belted kingfisher (male); Stephen McSweeny: ferruginous hawk; Patrick Moran: grass spider; Al Mueller: Cooper's hawk, sora; Jerry Oldenettel: American emerald, band-winged meadowhawk, blue-eyed darner, common green darner, common whitetail, flame skimmer, Paiute dancer, vesper sparrow, yellow-rumped warbler; D. Gordon Robertson: common yellowthroat (female); Mike Rogal: whitetailed deer (male); Cameron Rognan: American pipit, bank swallow; Ron Rowan Photography: white-breasted nuthatch; Alan Schmierer: fox sparrow; Shutterstock: American goldfinch, song sparrow, white-winged crossbill; Sergey Smirnov: bearberry; JW Stockert: hairy clematis; Stubblefield Photography: northern harrier (male), ruby-crowned kinglet, sharp-shinned hawk; Mark Summers: long-tailed weasel (winter); Michael J. Thompson: sage thrasher; Jerry Ting: warbling sparrow, white-throated swift; Tristanba: trashline orbweaver; Merlin Tuttle (Bat Conservation International): all bat images; Helena Van Dijk: snowshoe hare (winter); David Watkins: bobolink; Doug Waylett: Russula (emetica), goldenrod crab spider; Gail West: Wilson's phalarope (male); Michael Woodruff: golden-crowned kinglet; Yellowstone Public Domain Images: Steamboat and Echinus Geysers, pocket gopher; Eugene Zelenko: tule bluet.

Karen Kling lent her impressive artistic talents to create the following plates: all fish images, aquatic invertebrate images, and winter track images.

Acknowledgments

This book has been a labor of love that took almost ten years to develop. Along the way, many individuals and organizations contributed time, expertise, and resources to help make this a reality. Thanks to the following for their invaluable assistance.

Cheryl Jaworowski (Yellowstone geologist) and Anne Mattson (Grand Teton geologist) both provided wonderful feedback on the geology section. Researching mushrooms of the GYE proved difficult, and Dr. Bradley Kropp at Utah State University offered critical suggestions for appropriate species to include as well as accurate nomenclature. The plant section was reviewed by several botanists and was improved thanks to comments from my brother, Brent Johnson with the National Park Service, Dr. Matthew Lavin at University of Montana, and Amy Taylor with the Wyoming Native Plant Society.

The insect section was made possible with guidance from the following institutions and experts: Kevin Williams and Dr. James Pitts at Utah State University's Entomology Laboratory, Teton Science Schools' insect collection, Dr. Michael Ivie with Montana State University's entomology collection, the insect collection at Colter Bay Visitor Center in Grand Teton National Park, and Yellowstone National Park's Heritage & Resource Center.

During this book's development, I was fortunate to spend several days in the field with Dr. Charles Peterson from Idaho State University. His field expertise and taxonomic advice helped in the acquisition of reptile and amphibian photographs as well as in improving the species descriptions for the herpetology section.

Several regional experts provided feedback on multiple topics within this book that was enormously helpful. These included George Heinz (retired Yellowstone interpretive ranger), Katy Duffy (Yellowstone interpretive ranger), Dr. Susan Clark with Yale University, Sue Wolff (Grand Teton biologist), and Eric Cole (National Elk Refuge biologist).

One of the true highlights of working on this project was the opportunities that it provided to meet and learn from other like-minded naturalists. I am particularly grateful to have had the guidance from the following naturalists who provided both natural history suggestions as well as field guide authoring guidance: Bert Raynes (author of several GYE books), John Muir Laws (author of many California field guides), and Stuart Atchison (author of Southwest and Baja California guides).

Finally, I offer eternal gratefulness to my wife, Jill, and son, Torin, both of whom have endured many species-specific hikes related to this book and offered perpetual encouragement throughout this journey.

Index